The Open Air Cook Book

**For boat, tent, or caravan—
or barbecues at home**

by Nancy and Frederick Tingey

Frederick Tingey is the author of
Continental Car Holidays,
Europe on £50,
Camping in Europe and
Tackle Caravanning this Way

Charles Letts & Co Ltd
London Edinburgh and New York

Contents

Published by Charles Letts and Company Limited
Head Office: Diary House, Borough Road, London SE1 1DW

Jacket design: Ed Perera. Photograph: Peter Baker

Photographs: Frederick Tingey pp 42, 47, 59;
Calor Gas p 9
Illustrations: Ed Perera

First Published 1975

Standard Book Number: 85097 117 9

Printed in Great Britain

Introduction

Everyone accepts that living out of doors is no longer the primitive affair it once was. Nowadays, whether we take a caravan, a tent, or a boat, the equipment with which we escape into the open air can be highly sophisticated. This is particularly true of the equipment we use for cooking, which in scope if not size may well compare with what we have at home.

Yet too often it is assumed that the growing interest in food—for which Britons are rapidly gaining a reputation abroad—cannot extend to meals cooked out of doors. We hope to dispel this notion by indicating some of the culinary possibilities open to the thousands of people who cook in the open air: adventure and family campers, caravanners, small-boat sailors, and those who simply want to stage a barbecue out of doors. Good food is important and the kind of meals we prepare can make all the difference to a holiday. With the facilities most of us possess there is no reason why we shouldn't cook food as good as we can get in many restaurants—and at a fraction of the cost. But it would be silly to pretend that cooking out of doors doesn't have its limitations. Mostly, though, these are imposed by what you have to cook with. So we have grouped the recipes that follow not in the conventional egg-fish-meat order but according to the basic equipment with which you prepare them.

The recipes are as varied as we hope they are practical. They start from scratch and contain no hidden surprises. We give recipes for easily baked bread for those occasions when the shops are closed or are too far away, but none for pastry. If you have the facility of an oven it makes more sense to buy your pastry ready-made. And since cooking oil is messy to transport and deep frying is both impractical and possibly dangerous out of doors we have omitted any dishes that call for it. Sauté potatoes are usually an acceptable substitute for chips.

As most people will have at least one burner we have concentrated on dishes which can be cooked in one pan over one source of heat. Many of the recipes are interchangeable: with a two-burner stove you can if you like cook two one-burner meals at once; most dishes given for the barbecue can be cooked just as well over an open fire, and so on.

We make few references to convenience or tinned foods. They have their place, of course, when time is short or in an emergency, and some should be in every outdoor cook's larder. But how sad it would be, amid the splendour of nature, to sit down from choice to a meal of industrialised food.

We give handy measures for amounts like an ounce or half a pint but not their metric equivalents. To do so before Britain has gone fully metric would only lead to complications, we feel. But we have included conversion tables for use on the Continent now, and in Britain later on.

We shall be pleased if this book helps you towards enjoyable and successful cooking out of doors.

Getting in gear

With dozens of native bearers to carry it, Dr Livingstone took everything he needed and more when setting off on his treks through Africa. Nowadays, most of us have to be much more choosy about the kitchen equipment we take with us into the open air. Even if what we are able to buy is highly sophisticated and portable, we are still governed by the amount we can carry. So the more versatile a utensil is the more weight we save.

Caravanners and small-boat sailors have their basic equipment built in, though for them, as for car-borne family campers, there is a limit to what they can take. The choice is most critical for adventure campers, of course, for whom bulk and weight are all-important. Yet, if cooking is not to become a chore and the results indifferent, there is a certain amount of equipment you must have.

Most adventure campers cook and eat with little more than a tiny gas stove, nesting pans, camp kettle, knife, fork, and spoon. But without piling on the weight too much, there are other things which are well worth taking—like a trivet for grilling on an open fire.

Nesting pans with detachable handles, designed for outdoor use, are often too thin and easily become distorted. The more solid the pan the more evenly it conducts heat, while, off the heat, it keeps food hot longer, too. Heavier pans with fixed handles, admittedly not so easy to stow, are safer to use and less likely to burn or dry up the food cooked in them. Next best to these are nesting billies of heavy gauge aluminium each with an attached folding handle.

Every outdoor cook needs a deep frying pan with a well fitting lid and preferably a fixed handle. The more solid it is the better. A frying pan of this kind is one of the most versatile kitchen utensils imaginable, with which you can do much more than fry. You can braise, stew, dry-fry savoury and sweet pancakes, and even bake a pizza or a cake; and so long as you treat it right—by not overheating it, and oiling it after use—it doesn't have to have a non-stick coating, which wears anyway. (A non-stick coating often also puts up a barrier to the heat.)

Another basic need is a saucepan, again with a well fitting lid; and a steamer, or at least a double boiler for making sauces, to go with it. With this and the right kind of frying pan, you can cook almost anything.

For the outdoor cook an omelette pan is something of a luxury, but, if you insist on pancakes and a lot of egg dishes, choose one of about 8in diameter. If the pan is too large too few eggs get spread over too wide an area.

Sectional pans make the most of the heat from one burner but they tend to be unstable and their narrow, straight-sided shape makes it difficult to fish out the food. Better to take a larger and heavier saucepan to use for pot roasts. On most gas stoves too, when the burners are turned down low, they go out, so for simmering, an asbestos mat comes in very handy.

Heads of camping families who travel to sites by car should note that outdoor cooks cannot operate efficiently with the aching back that comes from bending too low over a stove. To cook comfortably a cooking table or stand at the proper height—like the Valor Romany camp kitchen we use, which takes a standard size two-burner stove with room to spare, has shelves above and below and folds down to a mere 30in by 14in by 2½in—is invaluable, and it weighs only 18lb. Diners cannot enjoy their meals, either, unless they are sitting comfortably on folding chairs at a folding table, again at the right height.

The two-burner stove you use on the cooking table may have a grill, but we do not find these particularly useful, and they also tend to waste gas by taking a long time to heat up.

The range of what you can cook is increased still further by a collapsible oven. One that has been on the market for a long time is the small Kubex, which folds down to 12in by 12in by 3in, and has one fixed shelf and two removable ones. It won't work as well as your oven at home—for one thing, it isn't insulated—but there is still a lot you can cook in it. Remember that since it is not self supporting, it can only be used on a two-burner stove.

A barbecue is great fun, whether you cook for two or twenty people; in the garden or on a camping site. We have a round Lucifer, which weighs only 9lb and comes complete with a foldaway stand and a spit for roasting above a grill area 13in across.

There are rectangular portable barbecues on the market, too, more convenient to use in that they have the spit at the side where drops of fat falling from the roast do not flare up on the coals, and, being rectangular—there is one with a packed size of only 17in by 13in by 4in—they take up less storage space.

Being the fastest method, pressure cooking is the most economical on fuel. Steam contains a lot more heat than boiling water, and why this method of cooking is so quick is because as the pressure of the steam builds up so does its temperature. The Prestige Skyline we take sailing or caravanning is no bigger than a medium size saucepan but is ten times more useful: for making stock or soup, for tenderising tough meat, for steaming whole chickens, or simply for cooking the harder root vegetables in a matter of minutes. Even though there is no advantage in using it to cook fish or green vegetables, we wouldn't go out of doors without ours—but we always make a point of taking a timer as well, for cooking times can be critical!

Every outdoor cook needs really sharp knives of different sizes for cutting up meat and vegetables, plus a means of keeping them sharp. Chopping is so much easier with a weighty and well balanced French cook's knife, with its bow-shaped blade curving to a point. A potato peeler, on the other hand, is more efficient than a knife, especially if it has a swivel action.

It may take a little longer, but with a really sharp knife you can cut meat almost as finely as it would be if you were able to mince it. A curved serrated knife is also useful for cutting into grapefruit and melons and for making visually attractive hors d'oeuvres.

Airtight containers for food storage are another essential, and so are mixing bowls shapely enough to be used for serving food in as well. Other items almost impossible to do without include egg whisk and separator, wooden spoon for sweet and savoury sauces, a palette knife for folding in egg whites, a grater for cheese and hard vegetables (ideally, free standing and made of stainless steel), a chopping board that can double as a pastry board, and solid screw-top containers for spillable liquids.

In summer especially, car-borne campers are also likely to find room for an ice box, and a hanging larder with insect-proof vents, for keeping food off the ground. The cooks of the family might also favour wire shelving on which to stack less perishable food inside the tent.

If like Dr Livingstone's your transport is of unlimited dimensions you can add to the list indefinitely. But two more items easily repay the space they take up: kitchen paper for draining fried food and for making washing up with little water less irksome, and aluminium foil—for the outdoor cook one of the greatest aids to improvisation that exists.

Many of the items on the following check list can, of course, be taken from home. The list is not intended to be exhaustive—nor to exhaust, by its weight, the outdoor cook, who will, of course, select from it only what he or she considers essential.

Equipment check list

aluminium foil
apple corer/potato peeler
asbestos mat
baking tray
barbecue
bottle opener/tin opener
chopping board
colander/salad basket
corkscrew
double saucepan
egg separator
egg whisk
fish slice/spatula
flour sifter
French cook's knife
frying pan with lid
grater-shredder
kettle
kitchen fork
kitchen paper
kitchen scissors
lemon squeezer
measuring spoons
mixing/salad bowl
omelette/pancake pan
oven
perforated spoon
pressure cooker
rolling pin
saucepan/lid/steamer
sieve
skewers
storage jars
wooden spoon

Making the most of what you have

Veteran adventure campers regularly cook piping hot three course meals on only one burner. They do it by heating their pans in relays so that the food they contain goes on cooking even after it has been taken off the heat.

Even if your equipment is much more extensive than this it pays to be just as miserly with fuel—and with the heat it generates, too. One way is to cook in a spot sheltered from the wind, another to clean the burners of your gas stove frequently, and to check that the air vents beneath them are clear. Yet another is to cover, whenever possible, every pan in which you cook.

One trick used a lot by professional cooks is to turn off the gas a few minutes before a dish is cooked and let the heat of the pan complete the process. Often, the heat inside the food itself is a help in this.

Always cook green vegetables in the minimum amount ($\frac{1}{2}$ to 1in) of water in a covered pan. If you like, cut them up small to reduce the cooking time. Cook harder root vegetables just as quickly, too, by grating them first. If you boil onions whole, make a cross cut towards the centre at the root end so that they cook from the inside out as well as from the outside in.

Covering the pan not only reduces cooking time, it also retains the vitamin C in the vegetables. Don't automatically throw the water away. It can be used for making a sauce.

People rarely treat vegetables with the respect they deserve—unless they are vegetarians, that is. Overcook them like most of us do and you ruin both their texture and their looks. Green cabbage, for example, needs to be cooked—in or out of doors—for no more than six minutes. Drain green vegetables immediately after cooking and using only the heat of the pan give them a more appetising appearance by tossing them in a little melted butter, or give them added flavour by cooking them in stock. And, for a change and to save time, cook two vegetables together in the same pan—onions and potatoes, young carrots and peas—cutting them up as necessary so that they are equal in size.

As any outdoor cook knows, different cooking methods give different textures and flavours to food. But seasoning is all-important, too. Salt not only stimulates the taste buds, it brings out the flavour of food as well.

If you're lucky enough to afford asparagus, cook the whole bundle, stalks down, in boiling water for a few minutes. Then cut the string and boil them in the usual way. By this method you avoid over-cooking the delicate tips.

Sometimes the end result repays being a little more generous with cooking times. Boil small potatoes in their skins and peel them when they're cooked. In fact, cook all root vegetables in their skins if you've time so that they retain their vitamin content and flavour. The gain in taste can be remarkable.

Since they're usually blanched before freezing, frozen vegetables need less cooking than fresh. If they happen to be peas or carrots, give them more savour by adding a little sugar to the water. When poaching fresh fish, improve the flavour in a different way by adding seasoning and a bouquet garni to the liquid. The best way to fry fish is to get the fat really hot and smoking to sear the outer surface and make it crisp. The same rule also holds good for meat and chicken. Once seared, it absorbs much less fat than it might otherwise do.

Use butter for frying freshwater fish to give them a much sweeter taste. But cook oily fish like herring and mackerel in their own fat.

Always dry first any food you sauté in a frying pan, and try not to crowd it or steam will build up round it to prevent it browning.

When frying chicken, cook it covered for the first 15 minutes, uncovered for the remaining five.

All the top chefs say we should brown meat at a high temperature and finish it at low. The smaller and thinner the meat the faster it should be seared to stop it drying out. Solid pieces of meat need long cooking over a low heat. Conversely, the smaller the pieces the greater the surface area you expose to the heat.

To extract the most flavour, brown meat and vegetables in a blend of butter and oil; butter to give a delicate sweetness to the food, oil to prevent the butter burning.

Put a stop to sausages bursting when you fry them by adding a few drops of water to the fat and covering the pan for a few minutes.

Meat that is cooked slowly is the most tender. But except in an old fashioned haybox there is little scope out of doors for long slow cooking. Second best to this is steaming in a pressure cooker, which has the added advantage of using the least fuel of all.

Grilling on a barbecue is also a fast way to cook—too fast, perhaps, until you've got the hang of it. The process is made even quicker by the skewers and spits on which you place kebabs and roasts conducting the heat into the food. Spit roasting is cooking at its best: what happens is that the air stops the meat from being softened by the steam produced by its own juices.

If you lack any particular item of equipment you may well be able to improvise something to take its place. Like using the bottle that contained the claret you drank with dinner last night as a rolling pin, or making the top part of a steamer do double duty as a colander.

Your saucepan may have a lid but no steamer, so up-end the lid, place poatoes or other vegetables in it, lay a thin cloth over them, bring the corners up over the top of the lid and tie them together—then return the lid to the pan. For improvising, though, there's nothing better than aluminium foil. You may not have a sectional frying pan yet you can easily convert an ordinary one with foil. Or you can use a lidless pan for braising by making a perfectly adequate cover from foil. Lay foil on a flat surface, too, to serve as a pastry or chopping board. Or use it to keep food hot. A boiled or baked potato, for example, tightly wrapped in foil, will keep hot for up to an hour.

Save cooking time and fuel, too, in the way you prepare your food. When you marinate meat for grilling the acid in the marinade helps to break down the connective tissue. This is an excellent way to preserve uncooked meat, too.

To get fish dry for frying is difficult. So we dip them in flour after making surface cuts along each side to make it easier for the heat to penetrate. We also save time by keeping handy in a jar ready seasoned flour, using a ratio of three parts flour to one of salt and pepper.

To avoid soaking dried fruit and vegetables, like apricots and beans, overnight, add them to boiling water, simmer them for two or three minutes then let them stand in the same water for an hour. After that cook them in the normal way. Planning menus in advance can save a lot of time especially when you are a long way from the shops. Cook twice as much of staple foods, like rice, potatoes, or pasta, as you need, keeping half for the following day.

The important thing when cooking out of doors is to be adaptable—in the way that suits you best. Even if you are restricted to only one burner, you don't have to juggle with pans. You might decide to change your eating habits instead, by cooking and eating meat and vegetables one after the other. After all, modest restaurants in France and Italy have been serving their food like that for years!

Buying and keeping food fresh

In warm weather especially, try to buy only what you need each day, of all perishable foods. In the open air fresh fruit, vegetables, or salad are generally easy to get hold of through local markets, or by visiting a nearby farm.

For outdoor cooks top quality meat is really the most economical buy. You can prepare and cook it more easily and there is not nearly so much waste. Most of us tend to be shy about asking the butcher for advice on what to buy, which is a great mistake. Usually he's only too pleased to make suggestions, and at the same time to prepare or cut up meat to suit the way you want to cook it—in inch-size cubes for kebabs, for example—at no extra charge.

The same goes for fishmongers, who will willingly clean and bone mackerel or any other fish you buy. If you're by the sea, don't forget that at low tide mussels, shrimps, and crabs are free for the finding.

Most chickens sold in shops are battery-reared broilers, only poor cousins to the tender and tasty birds that you can get only at a farm. Only from a farm too, is it usually possible to get fresh eggs from free range hens, or the kind of milk and cream that is now rapidly becoming just a memory. Inland sailors sometimes find that lock-keepers too are an invaluable source of supply. Remember, too, that in the right place at the right time, any fruit growing wild is yours for the picking.

Buy potatoes loose rather than prepacked: once they have been washed they won't keep for long. For flavouring buy tomato juice rather than puree, which often has a bitter taste. Italian tomatoes, with their slightly peppery taste, can only be bought in tins, and canned fruit and vegetables are the only ones, other than frozen, which provide an economic way of enjoying out of season food. So there's clearly a place for some tinned food in every larder. When buying canned meat, however, it pays to keep an eye on the price, for some of it can be as costly as fresh and yet have nothing of the taste or quality. Tea bags are easier to dispose of than tea leaves, and dried milk is a much better standby than tinned or long life. Sea salt crystals and peppercorns won't absorb moisture the way salt in granular form and ready ground pepper will and, more to the point, there's nothing to compare with the flavour of either when you grind them fresh in a mill each time you need them.

Living out of doors in summer the prime need is to protect food from insects and to prolong its life by keeping it cool—usually by ensuring that it is kept in the shade with air circulating freely all round it. Adventure campers based near a fast-flowing stream can preserve perishable food, like butter, by putting it into airtight containers near the water's edge and keeping it in place with a heavy stone. They can cool their milk and wine the same way by stringing the bottles at the neck to a nearby branch. A cloth wrung out in vinegar and wrapped round meat will protect it from flies and a good way of keeping cheese fresh is to hang it up wrapped in muslin. But outdoor cooks in other situations can store food in a cool and well ventilated larder almost as well as in a refrigerator.

In or out of the larder, keep all food well covered and wrapped. Plastic food boxes with tight fitting lids are ideal for foods like flour, sugar and anything else liable to absorb moisture, and airtight containers are essential for coffee, spices, and other highly flavoured foods. One or two cubes of sugar in the container will keep both cheese or biscuits fresh, but remember never to store biscuits together with cake or they will become soft.

Lengthen the life of lettuce by keeping it in a covered pan. Keep washed celery or chicory in a jug of water, or wrap in a wet cloth if unwashed. Store eggs in a cool dry place away from strong smelling food: if you are uncertain about the freshness of an egg a good test is that a fresh egg will sink to its side at the bottom of a glass of cold water, a less fresh one will tilt on its small end, a stale one will rise in the glass, and a bad one float. Use foil to store foods with incompatible flavours in the same container, but keep bread in a plastic bag.

Potatoes, milk and many other things deteriorate quickly if left in direct sunlight. Preserve milk in hot weather by boiling it, or cover it with a cloth and put it in a bowl of cold water where it will keep cool by evaporation. Butter keeps well if immersed in water, and so does cream when poured into a vacuum flask.

Butter that has gone rancid can be restored by dropping it piece by piece in fresh milk, leaving it for an hour then draining it and washing in water before patting it together again. Never keep fish-paste overnight without sealing it carefully by pouring melted butter over the entire exposed surface.

So long as you protect them from insects, dry packaged foods will keep well until they are opened, when they should be put in a storage jar with a tight fitting lid. In the open air a golden rule is to keep all food away from wasps and flies, the two most common carriers of disease.

Store cupboard check list

Flour, baking powder, dried yeast, cornflour, custard powder

Lentils, haricot beans, spaghetti, macaroni, rice, ground rice, dehydrated potato

Oatmeal, rolled oats, breakfast cereals, pearl barley, crispbread, crackers

Sugar, caster sugar, honey, jam, marmalade, syrup

Dried apricots, currants, raisins, prunes, glacé cherries, almonds

Bouillon cubes, yeast extract, anchovy essence, Worcester sauce, ketchup, Soy sauce

Olive oil, wine vinegar, mustard, salt, peppercorns, paprika, curry powder or paste, chili seasoning or powder, garlic, capers, gherkins

Tinned ham, frankfurters, beef, soup

Sardines, anchovies, tuna fish, pilchards, salmon

Tinned peas, green beans, broad beans, tomatoes, haricot beans, mixed vegetables

Tinned peaches, pears, pineapple, apricots, custard, rice, fruit juice

Dried rosemary, mint, thyme, bay leaves, basil, oregano, celery seed, allspice, cinnamon, ground ginger, nutmeg, cloves, caraway seed

Almond essence, vanilla, block chocolate, gelatine, lemon juice

Tea, coffee, powdered milk, evaporated milk, cocoa

Handy measures and quantities

Whether you cook them out of doors or at home, recipes are of two kinds—those in which the proportions may be critical—like sauces or soufflés—and those where another spoonful or two makes little difference to the outcome.

Most of the time, of course, it does not matter how you vary a recipe, by substituting an ingredient or by varying the amounts. Most of us try out a new recipe by following it meticulously the first time and then, more often than not, alter it to suit our own taste. This way our own individual style of cooking emerges, and is one of the secrets of the good cook. But for recipes in which precise proportions will make the difference between success and failure—an appetising dish or a glutinous mess—some method of proper calculation of amounts is unfortunately necessary.

Many cookery books refer to 'tablespoonfuls', sometimes specifying 'heaped' sometimes not. The question 'how much does a tablespoon hold?' echoes that hoary conundrum, 'how long is a piece of string?' Tablespoons vary in capacity, and by careful weighing we found that our own interpretation of 'heaped' differed by nearly half an ounce. Pursuing our researches we found that a 'teacupful' could vary as much as nearly a quarter of a pint and never came anywhere near the half a pint that some experts define it as. Finally, our level tablespoons equal six level teaspoons, not four as we are advised they should. You think the solution is to arm yourself with measuring spoons? We progressed to that thought too, and bought two or three different types. The variations here were so fascinating that we rang the manufacturers and asked on what type of spoon they were based. The reply we got was really quite satisfying; each has his own idea of what a measuring spoon should be, and manufactures accordingly!

Having read continually, of course, that old fable 'all measurements are based on the British Standard' we checked with the British Standards Institution. They told us that they could only 'recommend' their measurements, not impose them, and manufacturers were quite at liberty to produce any versions of their own.

What we do advocate, therefore, is that every outdoor cook who wants to measure accurately should try to buy the B.S.I. measuring spoons, which are stamped B.S.I. 1348 and bear the Institute's kite mark. We also recommend Stewart's cook's measure, of clear plastic, which gives British measures for liquids, and solids like flour and sugar, together with their metric equivalents.

Based on the B.S.I. measuring spoons the table below might be useful for calculating small quantities:

FOR ONE OUNCE YOU NEED:

1 level tablespoon	*2 level tablespoons*	*3 level tablespoons*
condensed milk	butter	cocoa
honey	cornflour	custard powder
jam	currants	flour
jelly	curry powder	grated cheese

1 level tablespoon	*2 level tablespoons*	*3 level tablespoons*
lard	raisins	ground rice
syrup	rice	semolina
treacle	sugar	shredded suet
	sultanas	

For ½ spoons divide down centre lengthways, for ¼ spoons divide again sideways.

3 teaspoons = 1 tablespoon   8 tablespoons water = ¼ pint
4 medium size oranges will give approx ½ pint juice
2-3 lemons will give approx ¼ pint juice

Outdoor cooks who regularly go camping on the Continent will have a head start when Britain has fully adopted the whole of the metric system. This is being introduced in stages, and this year we shall have to buy our sugar and salt in metric quantities, with metrication of other commodities following thereafter. We did not, however, feel it would serve any particular purpose to give metric equivalents for our recipes until the whole system has come into force.

The main unit of weight in Continental Europe is the kilo, which contains 1,000 grammes and is the equivalent of 2lb. 3½oz. When shopping for vegetables in a morning market in France, for example, you would ask for either a kilo (say 2lb) or a half kilo (say 1lb). When buying smaller quantities of other foods, as at a *charcuterie* (delicatessen) you would be more likely to call for 250 grammes (8½oz) or 125 grammes (about 4oz). For ready reckoning purposes 1 oz is usually calculated as 25 grammes. Converting British liquid measures to Continental is rather more complicated. The main unit of liquid measure in Europe is the litre or 1¾ pints (equal to 35 fl oz). A litre is made up of 1,000 millilitres (ml) [100 centilitres (cl)]. The centilitre measurement is, however, the one that is the most often used abroad. As an example, the average bottle of French wine holds 75 cl (around 1½ pints) while the half-bottle contains 36 cl (around ¾ pint).

More exact conversions are:

WEIGHT		CAPACITY	
g=*gramme*	kg=*kilogramme*	cl=*centilitre*	l=*litre*
1 oz	28.3 g	¼ pt	14.2 cl
4 oz	113 g	½ pt	28.4 cl
8 oz	227 g	¾ pt	42.6 cl
16 oz	454 g	1 pt	56.8 cl
1½ lb	681 g	1¼ pts	71.0 cl
2 lb	907 g	1½ pts	85.2 cl
3 lb	1.36 kg	1¾ pts	99.4 cl
4 lb	1.81 kg	2 pts	1.14 l
5 lb	2.27 kg	2½ pts	1.42 l
10 lb	4.54 kg	3 pts	1.70 l
		3½ pts	1.99 l
		4 pts	2.28 l

When shopping we have found that a useful guide (using rough metric equivalents) for amounts to buy per person is:

Soup:	½ pint (10 fl oz)
Fish:	on the bone 8 oz (200 g)
	filleted 6 oz (150 g)
Liver:	4 oz (100 g)
Meat:	with bone 8 oz (200 g)
	boneless 6 oz (150 g)
Onions:	4 oz (100 g)
Pastas:	2 oz (50 g)
Potatoes:	6 oz (150 g)
Rice:	for salad 1 oz (25 g)
	for Risotto or Pilaff 2 oz (50 g)
Dried fruit:	2 oz (50 g)

Should the mind go blank on metric conversions, the following doggerel could, perhaps, serve as a reminder:

A kilo you will need to know
Is two and one-fifth pounds or so

A litre can appear quite clear
One pint threequarters' pretty near

A kilometre foreign style
Is five-eighths of a British mile

For changing metres into feet
Four inches plus a yard is neat.

Hors d'oeuvres and salads

Whether hors d'oeuvres or salads are appetising or not depends on three factors, the raw materials you use, how you prepare them, and how you present them. In their own way they can turn out to be minor works of art—and you can eat them too! This success is well worth every minute longer you spend in choosing the right size tomato and the freshest lettuce and in working out the most attractive way of arranging contrasts of colour and flavour. A wide range of ingredients is usually available, more particularly in summer, of course, and on the Continent the early morning markets, with their abundant displays of freshly picked and locally grown vegetables and fruit, are fascinating places in which to shop.

Avocados—like olives, you either love or detest them: cut in half lengthwise, remove stone, dab with lemon juice to stop discolouration and serve with either a vinaigrette dressing or filled with cream cheese or shrimps.

Carrots: choose young ones, scrape and grate them raw, dress lightly.

Chicory (called endive abroad): is useful for its lasting crispness and is a good alternative to lettuce using the leaves whole or sliced. With the sharp point of a knife pushed into the base, cut out a v-shaped wedge (this is where most of the bitterness is concentrated).

Cucumber: rake it with a fork from end to end, then the slices you cut from it will have prettily indented edges.

Endive (called chicory abroad): is another alternative to lettuce, but does not go particularly well with anything else other than a French style green salad. It can be rather tough, so choose carefully, or use it as a hot vegetable by cooking it in boiling salted water.

Lettuce are of three kinds; round, Coz, and Webb, the last, more crisp and with less waste, being the best buy. Dry well after washing (put a few drops of Milton in the water if you're doubtful about its purity) by tossing in a wire basket or tea towel or patting gently with kitchen paper. (Unless the leaves are carefully dried the dressing will not adhere to them).

Mushrooms: trim the stalks, peel, wash and dry, and serve raw, finely sliced. This way they have a delightfully nutty taste.

Olives: an easy way to stone black olives is to insert a paper clip into them, turn it round and then pull it out complete with the stone.

Peppers: since the inner part is inedible, halve and carefully remove pips, core, and any pith. Slice very thinly.

Parsnips: peel, wash, and serve raw, shredded finely.

Radishes: top and tail, wash, and slice finely.

Tomatoes: make zig-zag cuts round the middle, pushing the point of the knife into the centre. Separate to produce two water-lily shaped halves. Alternatively quarter and sprinkle with parsley, or slice and serve separately, lightly sprinkled with chopped onion.

Turnips: peel, wash, and serve raw, either finely sliced or shredded.

Make salads more interesting by using tinned or pre-cooked vegetables, on their own, mixed with fresh salad, or combined with fruit, cheese, fish, meat, or eggs. Drain-dry tinned peas or green beans, dress with oil or vinaigrette; mix tinned asparagus with chopped hardboiled eggs and olives; sprinkle haricot beans with chopped parsley;

courgettes (carefully washed), boil and dress while still warm; peel and dice potatoes boiled in their skins and, while still warm, dress with mayonnaise and chopped chives; dice celery and apple, or cut celery sticks in half lengthwise, fill with a little mustard and cream cheese, or spread a little more cream cheese lightly along the cut edges, sandwich the halves together, then slice them crosswise; dice and mix pineapple, Cheddar cheese, and chicory; dice Cheddar and beetroot and mix with chopped olives; roll slices of ham around segments of melon, or stuff with cream cheese and sliced olives.

Canapés are fun to make and always look inviting. By using various combinations of a few basic ingredients you can achieve a resplendent effect. Try experimenting with four simple basics: cheese (cream or Cheddar), sliced tomatoes, hard boiled eggs and sliced cucumber. Set them out on separate plates and place two or three together on buttered crispbread.

Dips are one of the most relaxing and sociable ways to eat, and recall our primitive ancestors, who always sat round a communal pot! Dunk into them potato crisps, French bread or plain crackers, and crisp raw vegetables such as celery, cauliflower, etc.

Special Cheese Dip

serves 4

4 oz cream cheese
4 oz crumbled Roquefort or Blue cheese
¼ pint mayonnaise
1 tspn Worcester sauce

Mash all ingredients together and beat with a fork until the mixture is smooth and creamy.

Avocado Dip

serves 4

1 large avocado
4 oz cream cheese
1 tbspn lemon juice
½ level tbspn salt
Dash Worcester or Tabasco sauce
Pinch of paprika

Peel and mash avocado, add rest of ingredients, mix well and season to taste.

Salad dishes, either of one basic ingredient or a mixture of several, are particularly refreshing eaten in the open air. (Recipes for making mayonnaise, vinaigrette and other salad dressings are given on pp. 57-8)

Coleslaw

serves 4 to 5

1 small firm white cabbage
½ green pepper, *finely diced*
1 tbspn onion, *finely diced*
4 tbspns sour cream and mayonnaise mixed
1 tbspn sugar
2 tbspns wine vinegar
Good pinch celery and caraway seed
salt and pepper

Shred cabbage finely and soak in cold water for an hour or more until crisp. Mix vinegar and salt and pepper. Drain and dry cabbage and combine with vinegar mixture, stirring thoroughly. Leave for half an hour then add celery and caraway seed, green pepper, and onion. Mix in sour cream/mayonnaise dressing.

Salade Niçoise

serves 4

1 lettuce, *quartered*
4 firm tomatoes, *thinly sliced*
1 green pepper, *thinly sliced*
1 Spanish onion, *thinly sliced*
1 small tin tuna fish
1 hard boiled egg, *sliced*
1 tbspn capers
2 tbspns parsley, *chopped*
4 oz black olives
8 anchovy fillets

Arrange the salad in a bowl and toss in vinaigrette dressing. A dish that typifies the colour and savour of Provence.

Cucumber and Yoghourt

serves 6

1 large cucumber, *peeled and diced*
2 cloves garlic *(optional)*
¾ pint plain yoghourt
1 tbspn fresh mint, *chopped*
1 tbspn dried mint
salt and pepper

Easy to prepare and wonderfully refreshing on a hot day. Sprinkle cucumber with salt and set aside in a colander to drain for an hour. Crush the garlic with a pinch of salt, mix two tablespoons of yoghourt with the garlic, then add this to the remainder of the yoghourt and mix well. Add the fresh mint. Drain cucumber, cover with yoghourt dressing and decorate with dried mint.

Crab Cocktail

serves 4

4 oz tin crab meat
¼ pint mayonnaise
1 stick celery, *diced*
juice of 1 lemon
1 tspn tomato ketchup

Make sure you buy crab meat and not dressed crab. Remove the tiny pieces of cartilage from the crab meat. Mix crab, celery, and mayonnaise, and season with lemon juice and tomato ketchup. Arrange in individual glasses and chill if possible before serving.

Swedish Salad

serves 4

6 oz sausage (frankfurters or ham)
1 small lettuce
2 tomatoes, *sliced*
2-3 large potatoes
1 dessert apple
1 pickled cucumber

Boil potatoes in their skins, then peel and dice. Slice the sausages and mix with the potato, cucumber, and apple, and dress with vinaigrette. Serve on a bed of lettuce and decorate with sliced tomatoes.

Haricots with Cheese

serves 4

1 large tin haricot beans
4 oz Gruyère cheese, *diced*
3 tbspns vinaigrette dressing
½ tspn tarragon or sweet basil

An hour before serving heat the beans in salted water, drain and pour over vinaigrette dressing. Allow to cool. Just before serving mix in the Gruyère and sprinkle with tarragon. (You can also use tinned beans in tomato sauce, with the sauce washed off).

Waldorf Salad

serves 4

2 cups dessert apples, *peeled and diced*
salt and pepper
1 cup chopped celery
¼ pint mayonnaise
¼ tspn paprika

Mix well together. Variations: 2 cups sliced banana instead of apple; one cup sliced orange or pineapple and one cup apple; with or without grated cheese.

Ham and Egg Salad

serves 4

Small cucumber, *sliced*
4 slices ham
1 lettuce
1 dessert apple, *peeled and cubed*
4 hard boiled eggs
olives to garnish

Cover a dish with the washed and dried lettuce. Mix apple and cucumber and spread over the lettuce. Roll up slices of ham, pancake style, and lay on top. Surround with halved hard boiled eggs and garnish with olives.

Green Salad (French Style)

serves 4

1 heart of lettuce, *quartered*
1 bunch of cress
1 endive
3 leaves of chicory
2 tbspns parsley, *chopped*
2 tbspns vinaigrette dressing

Wash and dry lettuce, endive and chicory and pour over the dressing (using more mustard in the dressing than normally).

Russian Salad

serves 4 to 5

1 tin diced vegetables
2-3 flowerets of cauliflower
2 potatoes
¼ pint mayonnaise

Boil potatoes in their skins till tender, then dice. Boil cauliflower and cut into sprigs. Mix everything together, season and stir in only enough mayonnaise to very thinly coat the vegetables.

Mock Crab Salad

serves 4

1 lb white fish (cod, haddock, whiting, etc.)
4 oz Gruyère, *grated*
1 lettuce, *washed and dried*
4 oz shrimps
1 cucumber, *sliced*
¼ pint mayonnaise
1-2 tbspns white wine vinegar
½ tspn anchovy essence
1 tspn made mustard
salt and pepper

Steam fish, leave till cold then skin, bone and flake. Mix the cheese, mustard, anchovy essence and seasoning and beat in the vinegar. Arrange lettuce on outer edge of dish, line inner edge with overlapping cucumber slices, leaving centre free. Pile flaked fish in centre, cover with mixture of cheese and anchovy, then pour over the mayonnaise mixed with the shrimps.

Rice and Tuna Salad

serves 4

8 oz Patna long grain rice
4 tomatoes, *sliced*
$\frac{1}{2}$ cucumber, *peeled and diced*
$\frac{1}{2}$ green pepper, *diced*
1 small tin tuna fish
1 tbspn sliced olives, capers or raisins
2 hard boiled eggs, *sliced*
2 sticks celery, *diced*
1 dessert apple, *peeled and diced*
$\frac{1}{4}$ pint vinaigrette or thinned mayonnaise
1 tbspn parsley, *chopped*

Boil rice, drain, and dry. Stir in all ingredients except the tomatoes and enough dressing to moisten well. Pile in the centre of dish and surround with sliced tomatoes. Garnish with parsley. Instead of the tuna, use tinned salmon, or any flaked white fish.

Egg Mayonnaise

serves 4

4 hard boiled eggs
4 leaves of lettuce
4 olives
1 tin sardines
4 anchovies, *filleted*
2 tbspns mayonnaise

Halve eggs lengthwise and lay yolk down on lettuce leaves. Arrange the sardines between them. Garnish eggs with mayonnaise, anchovy fillets, and olive.

Simple Rice Salad

serves 2 to 3

4 oz rice
2 oz tinned peas
2 tomatoes
4 tbspns vinaigrette dressing
salt and pepper

Boil, drain, and dry rice. Skin and remove seeds from tomatoes, then mix them with the peas and rice and dress with vinaigrette. Season to taste.

Japanese Salad

serves 4

2 tomatoes, *peeled and diced*
2 slices pineapple, *chopped*
1 lettuce
4 tbspns cream *(double)*
1 orange, *peeled and chopped*
1 dessert apple, *peeled and diced*
Juice of $\frac{1}{2}$ lemon

Make a dressing by blending cream and lemon juice. Mix all ingredients except lettuce and bind with dressing. Serve on lettuce leaves or with lettuce cut in quarters.

Mimosa Salad

serves 3

1 orange, *peeled and in segments*
4 tbspns cream
4 oz grapes
2 bananas, *sliced*
juice of $\frac{1}{2}$ lemon
1 lettuce

Skin grapes and remove pips. Mix all ingredients except lettuce and then bind with dressing made with four tablespoons of cream and the lemon juice. Serve on lettuce leaves or with quartered lettuce.

Avocado Soup

serves 4

1½ pints beef stock, *chilled*
2 large avocados
½ pint single cream
salt and pepper

A delicious soup which needs no cooking. Pour the stock into a bowl and stir in the cream. Remove the skin and stone of the avocados and pass the flesh through a sieve, then stir in the stock and cream. Add salt and pepper to taste and chill if possible before serving.

Cold Andalusian Soup

serves 4

3 tomatoes, *sliced*
1 onion, *finely sliced*
1 small green pepper, *chopped*
2 pints vegetable stock
2 slices stale bread
½ cucumber, *peeled and diced*
2 tbspns olive oil
salt and pepper

A refreshing and nourishing soup eaten as a midday meal by the peasants working in the summer heat of Southern Spain.
Sprinkle the cucumber with salt and leave to drain with a heavy weight on top for half an hour. Soak the bread in water then squeeze as dry as possible. Place the onion in a large bowl, cover with half the tomatoes and the pepper, then add the bread, the cucumber and the remaining tomatoes. Add olive oil and lemon juice but do not stir. Pour the stock over gently and chill for two hours before serving, if possible.

Stuffed Cucumber and Tomato Salad

serves 4

2 hard boiled eggs
1 cucumber
6-8 lettuce leaves
4 oz ham, *finely diced*
2 tbspns mayonnaise
salt and pepper

Peel cucumber and cut in 3″ lengths. Scoop out most of the centre, leaving a little at one end to form a base. Skin tomatoes, slice off the top and scoop out the centres. Add tomato pulp (preferably sieved) to the ham, together with the mashed egg yolks. Mix in the mayonnaise and fill tomato and cucumber cases with the mixture. Arrange on lettuce leaves and sprinkle chopped egg white on the top.

Alternative fillings for either tomato or cucumber cases are diced mixed vegetables and capers; celery and apple in mayonnaise; cooked rice with grated cheese and chopped parsley/tomato pulp; cream cheese and chives mixed with a little tomato pulp or mayonnaise; sardines drained and cleaned and mashed in butter then mixed with oil and lemon juice; shrimps in mayonnaise; tuna or salmon in sour cream with a little made mustard.

Cooking on one burner

Cooking out of doors for the first time on only one source of heat, you could be forgiven for thinking that your diet would have to consist of nothing but bacon and eggs—served separately or together! But, on the contrary, by exploiting the potential of your basic equipment, you have scope for producing a wide range of dishes.

In this context we are not merely thinking of double and sectional saucepans or steamers—though these are invaluable if you have room to take them with you out of doors—for you can produce a hot two course meal, cooking several items separately, but simultaneously, in the same pan simply by enclosing them securely in aluminium foil.

The one burner cook's most important tool, we think, is the modest frying pan, particularly if it has a tightly fitting lid. This ancient utensil originated in Spain, where it it still widely used to cook a variety of traditional dishes, and not just fried food as often happens in Britain.

With a thick-bottomed frying pan you can cook not only a variety of casserole type dishes, but also, using the pan as a skillet, you can make drop scones, biscuits, cakes and even bread. In the same way, food cooked in the humble saucepan does not always have to be boiled. The more solid the saucepan the greater its potential for use in other ways.

The recipes that follow indicate the possibilities open to the one-burner cook using only these two basic items of equipment.

Fish Chowder — serves 4

A savoury fish stew from the Atlantic coasts of Canada and America, its name being derived from an Anglo Saxon mispronunciation of the French for cooking pot *(chaudière)*.

- **1 lb filleted white fish,** *skinned and diced*
- **4 oz salt pork,** *finely shredded*
- **1 lb new potatoes,** *sliced*
- **4 ripe tomatoes,** *quartered*
- **1 onion,** *chopped*
- **½ pint milk**
- **¾ pint water**
- **1 oz fat**
- **1 tbspn parsley,** *chopped*
- **salt and pepper**

Cook pork and onion in melted fat for 10 minutes. Add potatoes, tomatoes and fish and cook until golden. Pour on the water. Cover and simmer until the potatoes are tender (about 20 minutes) then add milk and simmer for another five minutes. Season to taste and serve sprinkled with parsley.

Stewed Haddock Fillets — serves 3 to 4

- **1 lb filleted haddock**
- **1 large tin tomatoes**
- **1 onion,** *sliced*
- **2 oz breadcrumbs**
- **juice of ½ lemon**
- **1 oz butter**
- **1 tbspn parsley,** *chopped*
- **salt and pepper**

Place the haddock in the pan with the tomatoes, onion, and parsley. Season well and add the lemon juice. Sprinkle the breadcrumbs over the top and dot with butter. Cover and cook gently for 20 minutes.

Creamed Fish

serves 4

$1\frac{1}{2}$ lb cod or haddock
$\frac{1}{2}$ pint milk
2 tbspsns Worcester sauce or
2 tbspns anchovy essence
2 oz butter
1 oz flour
1 pint water
salt and pepper

Wash the fish, add a teaspoon of salt to the water and simmer for 20 minutes. Remove to a side dish, reserving half a pint of the stock. Melt the butter, blend in the flour until smooth, and add the stock and milk. Bring to the boil, stirring continuously. Season with salt and pepper and add either the Worcester sauce or anchovy essence. Cook over low heat for five minutes while you skin, bone, and flake the fish. Add to the sauce and heat thoroughly.

A variation would be to cook the fish and then make a sauce by blending 4 oz butter, $\frac{1}{4}$ pint fresh cream, the juice of one lemon and a tablespoon of parsley, heated over low flame. Serve the fish in the sauce.

Tuna Pilaff

serves 4

8 oz Patna rice
12 oz tinned tuna fish, *flaked*
10 oz mixed frozen or tinned vegetables
2 sticks celery, *diced*
1 onion, *sliced*
3 tbspns soy sauce

You could, if necessary, use strongly flavoured stock in place of the soy sauce. Cook rice, drain, and put to one side. Strain oil from tuna into a saucepan and cook vegetables till tender but not brown. (Frozen vegetables will take slightly longer than tinned, of course). Stir in the rice, soy sauce and flaked tuna and cook gently until heated through.

Mussels in White Wine

serves 3-4

If you are camping near the sea, what could be more exciting than to collect mussels at low tide from places washed by clean sea water, and then cook them this French way (but never take them from stagnant or sluggish water).

4 pints mussels
$\frac{1}{2}$ pint dry white wine
1 tbspn onion, *chopped*
1 tbspn parsley, *chopped*
1 oz butter *(optional)*
$\frac{1}{2}$ oz flour *(optional)*

Scrub the mussels thoroughly, jerking them up and down to tug off the beards. Discard all that float or are slightly open and do not close immediately you put a little salt between the halves. Open any that seem too heavy in case they are full of sand. Check that each shell contains a mussel by trying to slide the two halves across each other; discard any that slide, for it means that the shell is empty.

Put the mussels in a large pan together with the wine, onion, parsley, pepper and salt. Cover and cook on a fairly high heat for about 5 minutes, shaking the pan occasionally to distribute the heat evenly. The mussels are cooked once they have opened. Serve them in soup plates. Either leave the stock for a moment or two so that any sand can settle on the bottom, or strain through a fine sieve, then add thickening (flour and butter) and ladle over the mussels.

Pot Roast

Set a solid saucepan with a well-fitting lid over a low heat and it is as good as a small oven.

Melt fat (dripping for beef, lard for pork) in pan put in the joint and regulate the heat till you can hear the meat sizzling gently. A 2 lb rolled joint needs about an hour to cook. After half an hour turn the meat and arrange potatoes, carrots, and onions around it. The vegetables should then be ready at the same time as the meat. Pour off excess fat and thicken with a little stock to make gravy.

Layer Meat Pudding

serves 3 to 4

A less complicated suet pudding, economical on meat and steaming time.

8 oz raw minced beef
2 large onions, *thinly sliced*
2 carrots, *grated*
½ pint rich stock
1 tspn parsley, *chopped*
8 oz flour
4 oz suet
¼ tspn salt

Mix flour, suet and salt together with enough water to form a not-too-stiff dough. Roll out and divide into four. Mix remaining ingredients for the filling and season generously. Put a layer of pastry into a greased basin, then a layer of filling and alternate until the basin is nearly full, finishing with a layer of pastry. Cover and steam for about 1½ hours.

Coq au Vin

serves 4

A famous French dish suitably adapted. Replace half the wine with chicken stock if you prefer, but don't expect the end-result to be as glamorous.

4 pieces chicken
3 lean rashers bacon, *diced*
1½ lbs small onions
¾ bottle red wine
8 oz mushrooms
2 tbspns brandy
¼ tspn thyme
1 bayleaf
1 clove garlic, *chopped*
2 tbspns olive oil
2 oz butter
½ oz flour

Brown chicken in the oil (in heavy pan). Remove to side-plate and pour off excess oil. Fry bacon, mushrooms and onions in half the butter, then add the chicken pieces. Pour in the brandy, and ignite it, shaking the pan till the flames subside. Put in the wine, bayleaf, thyme and garlic, bring to boil, cover and simmer on gentle heat for 45 minutes or until chicken is quite tender. Melt the remaining butter and make into a smooth paste with the flour. Add this little by little to the pan, stirring continuously until sauce thickens.

Economic Bacon and Potato

serves 4

1 lb potatoes, *peeled and diced*
4 rashers bacon, *diced*
1 pint stock *(chicken or beef)*
2 medium onions, *sliced*
1 tspn parsley, *chopped*
¼ tspn thyme

Cook bacon from cold; when it begins to fry, add onions and cook till golden brown. Add remaining ingredients, cover, and cook until potatoes are soft (about 20 minutes).

Sautéed Kidneys

serves 2 to 3

2 medium-size kidneys *(preferably calves)*
3 oz butter
1 bouquet garni
Juice of 1 lemon
salt and pepper

Core kidneys and remove skin and fat. Slice them thinly lengthwise. Melt 1 oz butter in pan and fry the slices over a moderate heat for about a minute each side. Put to one side, season and keep warm. Melt the remainder of the butter in the pan and add the herbs and lemon juice. Remove bouquet garni, stir well and pour over the kidneys.

Dublin Coddle

serves 4

A traditional Saturday supper dish in and around the Irish capital, seemingly dull to those who haven't tried it, it is, in fact, delicious. Few one-pan meals are easier to prepare.

1 lb sausages
3 large onions, *peeled and quartered*
4 large potatoes, *peeled and quartered*
¾ pint milk
2 rashers bacon, *diced (optional)*
¼ tspn pepper
salt to taste

Prick the sausages to prevent them bursting. Put all the ingredients in a large heavy saucepan with enough milk to more or less cover. Simmer gently for about 40 minutes, when the dish will be cooked and the milk will have turned into a sauce. Serve—and wait for compliments!

Jambalaya

serves 4

A visually interesting and savoury dish from New Orleans, where French and Spanish influences persist.

8 oz tinned ham, *diced*
6 oz prawns
8 oz Patna rice
1 green pepper, *diced*
1 onion, *sliced*
1 large tin tomatoes
2 oz butter
2 tbspns olive oil
½ tspn chili powder
¼ tspn thyme
¼ tspn marjoram
1 clove garlic, *chopped*

In a large pan, fry the pepper, onion, and garlic slowly in the butter and oil for a few minutes until soft (but not brown). Add the wine, tomatoes, herbs, and seasonings and bring to the boil. Scatter in the rice slowly, cover and simmer gently for 25 minutes. Mix in the ham and prawns and continue to simmer for another 5 minutes or so until the rice is tender. A teaspoonful of anchovy essence mixed in at this stage improves the flavour whether or not you are using the amount of prawns specified.

Chipolatas (8–10) can be substituted for the prawns and anchovy essence, in which case brown them first and cut into thirds. But the true Jambalaya is a combination of fish and meat, a point to be borne in mind if you decide to vary the combinations. Try chicken and haddock, for example.

Chili con Carne

serves 4

A well-known Mexican dish. The genuine Mexican red chili pepper is mild, not hot, and chili powder makes an ideal substitute.

1 lb lean beef or pork, *minced*
2 small tins tomato paste
1 tin (18-20 oz) red kidney beans
1 onion, *chopped*
$\frac{1}{3}$ pint of water
1 clove garlic, *(optional)*
2 tbspns chili powder
$\frac{1}{2}$ tspn basil
2 tbpsns oil or butter
salt and pepper

Tinned haricot beans could be substituted for the kidney beans, but it would be a pity because these are what the dish is all about. Cook onion and garlic in hot fat until golden brown. Raise heat and add meat, chili powder and basil and cook until brown, stirring frequently, then add tomato paste, water, salt and pepper. Cover and simmer gently for about 30 minutes. Add the beans and the liquid in which they are tinned, heat and serve.

Chicken Liver Risotto

serves 4

8 oz chicken livers, *chopped*
10 oz Patna rice
1 rasher fat bacon, *diced*
1 onion, *chopped*
1 pt chicken stock
1 tbspn grated Parmesan
2 tbspns oil or fat
1 tbspn fresh parsley, *chopped*
$\frac{1}{2}$ tspn basil
1 glass white wine

Fry the bacon and onion in the oil or fat until brown, then stir in the rice until it is well coated with oil. Add the stock, wine, and basil and cook gently for 20 minutes. Add the livers, mix well and cook for a further 4 to 5 minutes. Stir in the cheese and sprinkle the parsley on top.

Simple Steak and Kidney Pudding

serves 4

1 lb braising steak, *cubed*
4 oz kidney, *sliced*
1 onion, *sliced*
$\frac{1}{2}$ pint water or stock
4 oz self raising flour
2 oz shredded suet
1 oz fat
salt and pepper

Melt the fat over a high heat, roll the meat in flour, then brown it rapidly with the onion. Add the hot liquid and seasoning, cover and simmer for $1\frac{1}{2}$ hours. Mix flour and suet with water to make an elastic dough, shape into dumplings, and add to the meat. Simmer for 15 to 20 minutes more, adding additional stock if required. Adjust seasoning and serve.

Alternatively the dough can be rolled into a round a little smaller than the diameter of the pan and laid gently on top of the stew, but it needs to simmer for three quarters of an hour.

Irish Lamb Stew

serves 4

1 lb lean lamb
2 turnips, *sliced*
2 leeks or onions, *sliced*
1½ lbs small potatoes, *peeled*
1 lb carrots, *sliced*
1 pt stock
1 oz fat
6 peppercorns
2 tbspns lemon juice
1 bouquet garni *(optional)*
1 level tbspn flour
salt and pepper

Trim and slice the lamb and roll the pieces in seasoned flour, then brown in the hot fat. Pour on the stock, add seasonings, and simmer gently for 40 minutes. (A teaspoonful of yeast extract is as good as a meat cube). Add vegetables and cook for a further 30 minutes, or until meat is tender. Thicken if necessary.

Minced Beef

serves 4

12 oz lean minced beef
1 onion, *sliced or diced*
1 oz fat
½ pint stock
1 oz flour
salt and pepper

Lightly fry onion, add beef and cook for 5 minutes, then add the stock. Season and bring to the boil. Skim if necessary and simmer for 30 minutes. Thicken as necessary with the flour.

Chinese dishes can be adapted very successfully for one burner. Since any meat used is sliced very thinly, a little not only goes a long way but cooks quickly too. A secret of Chinese food is that the vegetables, also, are cooked for only a short time, to retain their crispness. But, whatever else one can do without when borrowing from the Chinese, two more or less essential ingredients are soy sauce and cornflour.

Chicken, Chinese Style

serves 2 to 3

8 oz boned chicken
2 oz mushrooms, *sliced*
½ green pepper, *sliced*
1 small onion, *sliced*
½ pint chicken stock
1 tbspn cornflour
2 sticks celery, *sliced*
½ white cabbage, *shredded*
1 tbspn soy sauce
1 oz fat
3 tbspns water

Cut the chicken into thin strips. Mix the cornflour with the water. Fry pepper and onion until tender but not brown, dip chicken slices in cornflour paste and add to the pan, frying for two minutes. Add celery, cabbage, and mushrooms together with the stock and simmer for 5 minutes (the vegetables must retain their crispness). Add soy sauce and thicken with the remainder of the cornflour paste. Cook for two minutes more.

Variations of this dish might be: pork with cucumber and courgettes or cauliflower; beef with onion, garlic, and green peppers—or green beans or peas with chives; kidney with 1 tbspn of brandy and a pinch of powdered ginger; or veal with 1 tbspn sherry or brandy. Any meat used should be finely sliced and dipped in cornflour paste before cooking.

Pork and Cabbage

serves 4

A commonplace title, perhaps, but one easier to pronounce than the original! The recipe has been modified here to reduce its cooking time. In fact, there are as many different names as there are versions of this appetising dish, popular in most Slav countries.

1 lb loin of pork, *finely sliced*
1 white cabbage, *roughly chopped*
6 peppercorns
½ pint sour cream
½ tspn caraway seed
2 tbspns vinegar or lemon juice
1 tspn thyme
1 clove
1 tbspn flour
salt and pepper

Put pork slices in pan with just enough water to cover, season, bring to boil and cook gently for 25 minutes. Wash the cabbage, cut into large pieces, add to pan with peppercorns, thyme, clove and caraway seed and simmer till cabbage is almost cooked. Add cream blended with flour and simmer for a further 10 minutes. Test seasoning and add vinegar or lemon juice.

Liver, Venice Style

serves 2 to 3

½ lb calves liver
1 lb onions, *thinly sliced*
½ pint dry white wine
½ lemon, *sliced*
1½ tbspn olive oil
salt and pepper

Cut the liver on the slant into thin slices no wider than a pencil. Cook the onions in the oil in a covered pan over low heat for 20 minutes, season lightly, add the liver and wine and cook for a further two to three minutes, turning frequently. Serve hot with slices of lemon. If you use any other kind of liver, simmer gently for 5 or 10 minutes more. (A traditional alternative to the wine and oil is butter and sage).

Pork Jardinière

serves 4

4 loin chops
1 large tin mixed vegetables
¼ pint stock
1 oz lard
1 tbspn flour
salt and pepper

Dust chops with seasoned flour. Brown quickly on both sides in melted lard. Stir in stock, cover pan and cook for 20 minutes. Stir in strained vegetables, heat for one minute and serve. A large tin of tomatoes can take the place of the mixed vegetables.

Pork, Hungarian Style

serves 4

12 oz salt pork
10 medium potatoes, *peeled*
8 small onions, *peeled*
1 oz butter
1 tspn thyme
1½ pints hot stock or water
2 oz flour
1 tspn parsley, *chopped*
1 bayleaf

Put stock on to heat. Cube the pork, brown it quickly in melted butter, put to one side. Stir flour into melted butter and cook until light brown. Stir in stock slowly, replace the pork, add potatoes, onion, and herbs. Simmer for 45 minutes, or until pork is tender.

Beefburgers

serves 4

12 oz lean minced beef
2 oz fat
5 oz breadcrumbs
1 tbspn diced onion
1 small egg
3 tbspns cold water
salt and pepper

Cook onions in melted fat, but do not brown. Remove, allow to cool, and mix all the ingredients in a basin. Divide into four and shape into balls, using a little flour, then flatten the balls into rounds. Fry on each side until cooked right through.

Noodles Normandy Style

serves 4

12 oz noodles
4 oz mushrooms, *sliced*
6 oz bacon, *diced*
1 oz butter
3 tbspns cream
salt and pepper

Cook the bacon and mushrooms quickly in the butter, then set aside. Boil noodles until tender, drain and return to pan. Add bacon and mushrooms and heat carefully for a minute or two. Remove from heat, mix with cream, season to taste and serve.

Spanish Omelette

serves 2

4 eggs
1 small onion, *chopped*
2 ripe tomatoes, *quartered*
1 tbspn water
1 clove garlic, *diced*
½ green pepper, *chopped*
3 tbspsns oil
salt and pepper

Brown the vegetables in the hot fat, turning occasionally, for 5 minutes. Allow to cool. Beat eggs lightly with a fork, add water, salt and pepper and pour over the vegetables. Tilt pan so that liquid is spread evenly. When the eggs begin to set turn the omelette to brown the other side.

Savoury Pancakes

serves 2

1 cup flour
1 cup water
1 or 2 eggs *(depending on size)*
4 oz ham, *diced*

Mix all ingredients to a smooth batter. Pour 2 tablespoons into previously greased and heated pan, tipping to make batter run thin and level. Fry on one side only and when set put aside and continue with rest of batter, putting one pancake on top of the other with a sheet of greased paper between for easy separation. Place a tablespoon of ham on the cooked side of the pancake, fold over, and fry on both sides. Other suggested fillings: grated cheese, grated onion, chopped liver sausage, diced frankfurters.

Beans, Italian Style

serves 4

2 lb fresh green beans, *sliced*
1 lb tomatoes, *quartered*
1 onion, *sliced*
1 cup stock
1 oz fat
2 cloves garlic, *sliced*
1 bouquet garni
1 tbspn chopped parsley
salt and pepper

Melt the fat over a moderate heat and quickly cook the tomatoes, onion, and garlic. Add stock, beans, bouquet garni, and seasoning. Lower the heat and cook very gently for 20 minutes. Serve with a knob of butter and the parsley.

Potatoes, Lyonnaise Style

serves 4

2 lb potatoes, *peeled and quartered*
3 onions, *sliced*
½ pint dry white wine
2 oz butter
1 oz flour
salt and pepper

Melt butter in pan and brown potatoes and onions. Add the wine blended with the flour and seasoning. Mix well, cover the pan and cook over low heat for 30 minutes, or until potatoes are soft.

Peas, Parisian Style

serves 4

2 lb fresh peas
2 carrots, *sliced*
1 tbspn parsley, *chopped*
1 cup stock
1 oz butter
2 onions, *one sliced, one stuck with a clove*
1 clove garlic
several lettuce leaves
salt and pepper

Melt the butter and cook the sliced onion. Add the whole onion stuck with a clove, the carrots, peas, lettuce, garlic, parsley and stock. Season and cook for 25 minutes.

Bread without Yeast

6 oz self raising flour
¼ pint milk *(preferably sour)*
1 level tbspn baking powder
2 tbspns oil
1 level tspn salt

Sieve the flour into a bowl, dissolve the salt and baking powder in the milk, and use enough of the liquid to make a loose dough. Divide in two and dust with flour. Melt the oil in a deep 8 in. diameter omelette pan over moderate heat, then put in half the dough, pushing it out with the fingers to evenly cover the pan. Cover and cook over moderate heat. When the underside has browned (about 10 minutes) turn out (invert a plate over the top), butter the pan again and cook the other side. Repeat for the remaining dough. (Each crusty loaf can rise to a height of 2 in. or so. The bread, which has more flavour if sour milk is used, is best eaten hot, with plenty of butter).

Raisin Cake

4 oz self raising flour
3 eggs, *separated*
1 oz butter
½ cup water
4 oz caster sugar
½ cup raisins
1 tbspn rum
1 oz glacé cherries

Melt half the butter in a heavy frying pan over moderate heat. Rub the remaining butter into the flour and mix quickly with the sugar, egg yolks, raisins, rum and water. When the butter is smoking pour half the mixture into the pan. Cover and cook over a low heat for 10 minutes, then turn out, butter the pan again and brown the other side. Do the same with the remainder of the mixture. Beat the egg white with a little sugar until stiff, spread over the cakes and decorate with cherries.

Perigord Biscuits

3 oz plain flour
1 oz butter, *melted*
2 oz sugar
1 tbspn rum
1 egg
¼ tspn salt
2 tbspns water

Sift dry ingredients into a bowl and make a well. Blend in egg, rum, half the butter and the water. Knead into stiff dough, roll out to thickness of ¼ in. and cut into fingers. Roll in flour and brown each side in hot butter over moderate heat in covered pan. (10 minutes).

Scotch Pancakes

makes 12

8 oz self raising flour
2 oz caster sugar
1 oz butter, *melted*
1 oz fat
1 or 2 eggs (*depending on size*)
½ pint milk
salt

Sift flour, sugar, and salt into a bowl. Beat the eggs and mix them with the milk. Make a well in the centre of the flour and pour in egg mixture and melted butter. Beat until smooth. If necessary add more milk so that the mixture runs easily off the spoon. Grease thick frying pan (or griddle) and when hot drop in a tablespoon of the batter. When bubbles appear on the surface of the pancakes turn them before they burst, or the scones will be too dry. Grease pan between batches. Serve with jam, butter or syrup.

Pancakes

serves 2

4 oz plain flour
2 eggs, *separated*
1 oz butter, *melted*
½ pint milk
1 oz fat
pinch of salt

Make the batter at least an hour before using. Beat yolks and then whites of egg separately. Sift flour and salt into a basin, add yolks and whites and beat till smooth. Add milk gradually and beat again. Just before cooking add 1 tablespoon of melted butter. Put a knob of fat into the pan, swirl it around to coat the sides and drain off any surplus. Pour in enough batter to thinly cover the bottom of the pan, and toss or turn as soon as underside is brown. Serve with lemon and sugar, or jam. (A quick way of greasing the pan between pancakes is to have some already melted fat nearby and to spoon it in as necessary).

Apple Fritters

4 oz flour
¼ pint milk
2 cooking apples
1 egg, *well beaten*
½ oz butter, *melted*
¼ tspn salt

The batter should preferably be left to stand for an hour after making, but if you want to use it immediately mix as gently as possible or it will not adhere to whatever it is intended to coat.

Sift salt and flour. Add egg and beat till smooth. Stir in melted butter, beat the milk in gradually and continue beating till the mixture is smooth. Core, peel and slice apples fairly thinly. Sprinkle with a little caster sugar and lemon juice and leave for 10 minutes. Drain, dip in batter and fry. Make banana fritters in the same way.

Steamed Apples

serves 4

4 cooking apples, *cored but not peeled*
1 oz butter
¼ tspn cinnamon
2 oz brown sugar
½ cup raisins

Score the skin round the centre of each apple and fill centres with the butter, sugar, and raisins spiced with cinammon, then wrap in foil. Place in steamer for 25 minutes or more, depending on size of apples.

Apple Crumble

serves 4

1 lb cooking apples, *peeled and sliced*
2 oz caster sugar
4 oz flour
2 oz butter

Rub fat into flour and mix in sugar. Put on top of apples and steam for 30 minutes, covered. Serve with tinned custard or cream.

The open fire

Man cooked his first meal over an open fire. So it shouldn't surprise us that the tang of woodsmoke can strike an ancestral chord in the most sophisticated city dweller.

Eating freshly cooked food beneath the stars by the flickering light of burning logs creates a wonderful backwoods atmosphere, cheerful yet exciting to adults and children alike.

Unfortunately an open fire is banned in many areas and often where one is allowed there's little or no wood to be had. Yet there are places, even in overcrowded Britain, where you can build a fire: in mountain areas below the tree-line, on deserted beaches and, with permission of course, on farmland.

Avoid pebbly beaches, though. When flints get hot they are liable to explode with a bang. Other stones may do the same when wet. Avoid areas strewn with leaves, dry grass or dead bracken, too, on which a fire can easily get out of hand.

Be extra careful in dry windy weather and never leave a fire unattended. Observe the County Code, of course, taking care not to damage live trees and to remove all traces of your fire before you leave.

Where you do have a choice, use fast-burning wood to get the fire going, then follow this with hardwoods such as beech, ash, or holly—all of which make little smoke. (Elm, the wood most common in Britain, does not burn well).

Build your fire inside two thick green logs or rows of dry flat stones in line with the prevailing wind. The virtue of a long narrow fire for cooking is that it is easy to control, produces embers quickly and makes the most efficient use of the heat by directing it upwards. Before lighting it, collect more dead wood than you think you are likely to need.

For cooking you want not flames but a sizeable bed of embers which will last for as long as you intend to cook. Since most wood takes about two hours to burn down to embers suitable for cooking, meals prepared over an open fire are not for those in a hurry.

Place the logs or stones close enough together to take a row of pans or a trivet for grilling. Use the windward end of the fire for fast cooking and boiling water, the downwind end for food that needs a lower heat. Feed the fire at the windward end and rake the embers along as necessary.

Push Y-shaped sticks into the ground on either side to take a crossbar for roasting. Or prepare and season food, wrap it securely in a double thickness of foil and bury it in the embers, where it will cook in its own steam.

Or sharpen some green non-resinous sticks (such as willow) with which everyone can grill his own sausage or piece of meat over the fire, or spear chunks of bread and dip them in a gently bubbling fondue, a dish fascinating for children.

With the right kind of fire you can cook in a variety of other ways too: grill meat or fish on a trivet or bake unleavened bread twisted round a stick and placed spit fashion over the fire or pushed into the ground at an angle.

One problem about cooking in foil is that apart from opening the package you have no way of knowing if the food is ready. Unless you time it, that is.

Yet cooking in foil has many advantages. The food will not dry up (provided it is properly sealed in) and it can be served in the foil in which it was cooked, so saving washing up.

Use foil double thickness, fold it over the food, even up the edges and turn them two or three times towards the centre in $\frac{1}{2}$ in. folds, then press the folds flat. When the food is cooked, open the envelope by cutting into one side, leaving the other intact to serve as a plate. You will probably need to practise several times, though, before you learn how to make an effective seal.

What you are able to cook depends, of course, on the kind of fire you are able to build and the equipment you use. The recipes that follow merely indicate some of the possibilities.

Corn on the cob. Insert a skewer into each end of the corn, brush with melted butter and grill over fire for about 20 minutes. Turn frequently, brushing occasionally with more butter.

Baked potato. Wash large potatoes and while still wet coat with salt. Cook uncovered in embers for 1 hour or more. Baked in this way they have a unique flavour. When they are cooked, cut in half lengthwise and serve with a dressing of plain yoghourt, chopped chives, salt and pepper.

Fish in foil. A method best suited to whole fish like medium size trout. Clean the fish and score them along the sides with a sharp knife. Season inside and out and sprinkle with lemon juice. Cover and cook for about 20 minutes.

Chops in foil. Lay each chop in a separate piece of foil. Add a knob of butter; season and sprinkle herbs (thyme, rosemary, or basil) on top. Wrap foil loosely but make a double fold at each edge. Bury in embers for 30 minutes or more.

Herrings in oatmeal — serves 4

4 large herrings
1 oz butter
2 oz oatmeal
$\frac{1}{2}$ lemon, *sliced*
1 tbspn parsley, *chopped*
salt and pepper

Bone the herrings and remove the heads and tails. Clean by rubbing with salt, then wash and dry. Season with salt and pepper and coat with oatmeal, pressing it well into the flesh on both sides. Fry in melted butter until brown (about 15 minutes), turning once. Serve with lemon and parsley.

Devilled chicken — serves 4

4 chicken legs
4 tbspns olive oil
2 tspns tomato ketchup
$\frac{1}{2}$ tspn curry powder
2 tspns made mustard
2 tspns vinegar
$\frac{1}{2}$ tspn black pepper
pinch cayenne pepper

Place chicken on trivet over fire and cook for 10 minutes each side. Allow to cool then remove skin. Mix oil and curry powder into a smooth paste, add the remaining ingredients and brush the mixture generously over the chicken. Return it to the fire and cook for about 25 minutes, turning and brushing occasionally with the sauce.

Beef stew

serves 8

2 lb lean chuck steak, *cubed*
1 large tin Italian tomatoes
1 oz beef dripping or lard
4 potatoes, *quartered*
2 onions, *quartered*
6 carrots, *sliced*
½ cup red wine
1½ cups water
2 tbspns flour
2 tspns salt
¼ tspn pepper
2 bay leaves

Roll the meat in seasoned flour then brown it in the hot fat. Add the carrots, tomatoes, onions, water, wine, herbs, and seasonings and simmer for 1 to 1½ hours. Add potatoes, cover and cook for a further 30 minutes. Thicken the sauce by blending the remaining flour with ½ cup water.

Beefburgers

serves 4

1 lb lean minced beef
2 onions, *chopped*
1 tbspn parsley, *chopped*
1 oz beef dripping or lard
salt and pepper

Mix the onion and parsley thoroughly with the meat and shape it into four flat cakes about ½in thick. Cook for 15 minutes each side on greased foil, drain and serve American-style between soft bread rolls.

Cheese fondue

1 lb Cheddar cheese, *grated*
½ bottle dry white wine
1 clove garlic, *crushed*
2 oz butter
½ tspn cornflour
½ tspn dry mustard
salt and pepper

Cream the mustard and cornflour with the garlic and half the wine. Melt butter in heavy pan, tilting it so that the liquid coats the sides. Add the cheese and the remainder of the wine, stirring continuously until smooth. Add the cornflour and mustard mixture and cook for three minutes, stirring all the time. Season and simmer gently (do not let the mixture boil), stirring occasionally. If you like, use dry cider instead of wine and equal quantities of hard and soft cheese in place of Cheddar. Everyone helps himself to fondue by dipping into it cubes of bread on a fork.

Quick bacon and potato

serves 2

½ lb potatoes, *peeled and sliced*
1 oz bacon, *shredded*
½ pint stock
1 small onion, *sliced*
¼ tspn parsley, *chopped*
¼ tspn thyme

Fry the bacon with the onion until golden brown, add the remaining ingredients and cook until potatoes are soft.

Sausage and tomato ragout

serves 4

8 skinless pork sausages
1 onion, *thinly sliced*
1 green pepper, *seeded and chopped*
1 large tin Italian tomatoes
1 oz butter
1 tspn Worcester sauce
1 cup water
salt and pepper

Fry onion and pepper until tender, cut the sausages into pieces and cook until browned. Add the tomatoes and water and stir until the liquid boils. Add the Worcester sauce and seasoning and simmer for 15 minutes.

Pan-baked Pizza

serves 2

6 oz flour
2 tspns baking powder
1 cup water
1 small tin Italian tomatoes
1 oz Cheddar cheese, *grated*
4 tbspns olive oil
½ tspn oregano or basil
4 anchovy fillets
salt and pepper

Mix flour, salt, and baking powder together, then add as little water as possible to make a stiff dough. Knead lightly, then roll or pat out to a round about 8in across. Heat half the oil in an 8in diameter pan, put in the dough and cook over a low heat for 5 minutes. Turn, cover with the tomatoes, season with salt and pepper, and top with the anchovies then the cheese. Sprinkle oregano or basil over the cheese and pour on the remainder of the oil. Cover pan and cook for another 5 minutes.
Make this in a larger pan by increasing the quantities of flour, baking powder and salt: for best results, the dough must wholly fill the pan.

Garlic bread

serves 4

1 French loaf
2 oz butter
2 cloves garlic, *crushed*
salt and pepper

Make diagonal cuts in the bread every 1½in from one side almost through to the other. Season the butter, mix with the crushed garlic and spread between each slice. Then reshape the loaf and wrap tightly in foil. Place in the embers or at the edge of the fire for about 15 minutes.

Griddle bread

serves 6

8 oz flour
2 tspns baking powder
1 tspn salt
½ cup water

Mix flour, baking powder and salt together, then work in enough water to make an elastic dough. Knead thoroughly and shape into thin rounds. Place on trivet over fire, wait until bread begins to rise then turn and cook for 5 minutes more.

Cinnamon apple

serves 4

4 large cooking apples
4 tbspns raisins
1 oz butter
4 tbspns brown sugar
¼ tspn cinnamon

Core apples (leave unpeeled) and make a cut round the centre of each. Fill centres with raisins sprinkled with sugar and cinnamon and top with knob of butter. Rub butter round outside of each. Bring foil loosely up round each apple and seal by twisting tightly together the ends at the top. Bake covered in hot embers for 20 minutes.

Cooking on two burners

The cook who acquires the use of two burners after having had to make do with one may at first be at a loss to know how to make the most of the second source of heat! But it doesn't take long to recognise the possibilities: to fry or stew on one burner while boiling water or steaming vegetables or a dessert on the other; to cook two one burner dishes at once or even staples like rice or potatoes to get ahead on a meal for next day; or to serve three course meals for special occasions. The greatest advantage of having two burners is that one can cook more elaborate meals.
The recipes that follow fall into two categories: dishes in which the components parts must be cooked separately even though they are blended together at the end, and those in which meat and vegetables, for example, remain separate both during cooking and serving.

Kedgeree

serves 4

8 oz Patna rice
2 eggs
1 lb smoked haddock
4 oz butter
½ tspn lemon juice
1 tspn parsley, *chopped*
1 tspn curry powder
pinch grated nutmeg
salt and pepper

BURNER 1. Hard boil the eggs, cooking haddock in steamer over the water for ten minutes. Skin, bone and flake the fish and slice the eggs, cutting them in half lengthwise first.
BURNER 2. Cook the rice then put to one side. Melt the butter, stir in curry powder, lemon juice and seasonings and cook very gently for a few minutes. Mix in egg, flaked fish and boiled rice. Serve sprinkled with parsley.

Lamb Curry

serves 4

1 lb lamb, *cut in small pieces*
1 medium onion, *sliced*
1 cooking apple, *sliced*
1 small tin tomatoes
1 tbspn curry powder
1 tbspn sultanas
1 tbspn syrup
½ pint stock, meat cube, or 1 tspn yeast extract
1 oz fat

BURNER 1. Heat the fat and fry the onion and apple. When they are about to turn colour, put in meat and brown all over. Add the rest of the ingredients (curry paste, if you have it, will produce a better result than curry powder) and simmer slowly until the meat is tender (45 minutes or more).
BURNER 2. We always use a brand-named long grain (Patna) rice as it does not need to be washed before cooking and always gives good results. One cup of uncooked rice will expand to three cups when cooked. Keep to the ratio of one cup of rice to two cups of water, with half a level teaspoon of salt to each cup of rice. Boil the water, sprinkle in the rice, lower the heat, cover and simmer gently for about 15 minutes, when all the water will be absorbed and the rice will be cooked. Fluff up with a fork. A little oil dropped in the water while the rice is cooking should prevent it sticking to the bottom of the pan. It

helps to separate the grains too.
Chapatis are often eaten in place of rice in India, and are simple to make. Mix up a dryish dough from wholemeal flour, salt, and water. Roll it out thinly, cut in rounds using a small saucepan lid, then flour the chapatis and cook over a moderate heat in a dry frying pan—use no fat at all. Paratas are made in the same way, except that they are buttered before being cooked to a golden brown.

Russian Stew with Meatballs — serves 4

We first ate this dish years ago in a Russian restaurant in Paris and were so impressed that we sought out the chef and humbly asked how he had prepared it. He was so delighted by our interest that he insisted on giving us the recipe, along with that for Boeuf Stroganoff, given later in this section.

1 lb mushrooms, *sliced*
½ lb minced beef
1 pint hot stock
3 oz breadcrumbs
1 onion, *finely sliced*
2 tbspns lemon juice
3½ oz butter or other fat
1 bayleaf
2 tbspsns flour
salt and pepper

BURNER 1. Melt 2½ oz of fat over a moderate heat and cook the mushrooms for 5 to 6 minutes. Stir two tablespoons of flour into the fat in the pan. Add stock, lemon juice and seasoning and bring to the boil, stirring all the time. Simmer for 5 minutes.
BURNER 2. Soak the breadcrumbs in a little water then squeeze out excess moisture. Cook the onion gently in an ounce of butter, remove from heat and mix with the meat and breadcrumbs. Season and roll into little balls the size of the top half of your thumb. Brown them, add to the mushrooms and stock and simmer for another 10 to 15 minutes. When you have transferred to one pan cook a green vegetable on the second burner, such as cauliflower, thinly sliced white cabbage (boiled for only 5 minutes to keep it crisp) or broccoli.

Spaghetti Bolognaise — serves 4

Pasta is a generic term for the bewildering variations with beautiful names like *tonnelini, chiocciole, trenette,* and *tagliatelli,* all shaped differently but all tasting the same. What makes each dish different is the sauce served with it, of which there are infinite variations, although many people prefer a meat sauce with spaghetti.

½ lb spaghetti
½ lb beef, *minced*
¼ lb lean pork, *minced*
1 large tin tomatoes
½ tspn basil
1 small tin tomato paste
3 oz grated Parmesan cheese
2 oz butter
2 tbspns olive oil
1 clove garlic, *chopped*
pinch paprika
½ pint water
1 onion, *sliced*
salt and pepper

BURNER 1. Heat oil and fry onion and garlic, then meat. Cook, stirring for a few minutes, then add tomatoes, tomato paste, basil and seasoning. Cover pan and cook gently for 20 minutes or more. (The longer the cooking the better the flavour. Add further water if required).
BURNER 2. Drop spaghetti into at least a quart of boiling salted water and cook in an open pan for 12 to 15 minutes. After the first 10 minutes

test by tasting. Properly cooked, spaghetti is tender yet resistant to the teeth *(al dente* in Italian). Strain, dot with butter, and pour over the meat sauce. Serve sprinkled with Parmesan cheese.

Chicken Maryland

serves 4

4 pieces frying chicken
4 bananas
2 eggs
1 tin sweet corn
2 oz butter
1 oz breadcrumbs
2 tbspns milk
¼ pint water
pinch salt
4 oz flour

Mix flour, salt, water, and one of the eggs to make a stiff batter.
BURNER 1. Egg and breadcrumb the chicken and fry in butter till golden brown.
BURNER 2. Drain corn and put into batter, then drop tablespoon by tablespoon into hot fat. Fry each side till light brown. Put to one side. Peel bananas, dip in milk then flour and fry sufficiently just to brown.

Savoury Noodles

serves 4

1 lb sausages
8 oz noodles
8 oz mushrooms, *sliced*
1 green pepper, *diced*
1 large tin tomatoes
½ tspn basil
1 onion, *chopped*
2 tbspns tomato paste
½ pint chicken stock
1 tspn chili powder
½ tspn thyme
8 black olives, *sliced*

BURNER 1. Cook sausages until brown, remove from pan, leaving fat, and put in mushrooms, onion and pepper and fry for 5 minutes. Add stock, tomatoes, tomato paste, herbs, and seasonings and simmer for 10 minutes, stirring frequently. Replace sausages in pan and heat through.
BURNER 2. Drop noodles into a large pan of salted boiling water and cook till tender (about 8-10 minutes). Drain, add sliced olives and mix with meat.

Kidneys in Cream

serves 4

8 lambs' kidneys
½ pint beef stock
2 tbspns sour cream
3 oz butter
1 oz flour
salt and pepper

French Beans Provencale

serves 4

1 lb French runner beans
1 small tin Italian tomatoes
2 tbspns oil
1 clove garlic, *crushed*
1 tbspn parsley, *chopped*

Soak kidneys in cold salted water for half an hour. Dry, remove core, and slice thinly. Top, tail, and string beans and cut into short lengths on the slant.
BURNER 1. Heat butter and fry kidney slices for 5 minutes. Stir in flour, then add stock slowly. When it has thickened simmer over low heat. After 10 minutes add sour cream and seasoning and cook for a further five minutes, stirring continuously.
BURNER 2. Drop the beans into boiling salted water and cook for 10 minutes. Drain. Heat oil in pan, add the beans, garlic and tomatoes. Stir over low heat for 5 minutes. Add parsley and serve.

Gammon with Pineapple

serves 4

4 gammon steaks
small tin pineapple slices
½ cup chicken stock
1 tbsp tomato paste
1 dspn cornflour
Fat for frying

Courgettes, Italian Style

serves 4

1 lb courgettes, *washed and sliced*
1 onion, *thinly sliced*
1 bouquet garni
1 tbspn oil
¼ pint stock or water
salt and pepper

BURNER 1. Fry steaks slowly in a little hot fat till brown on each side. Put to one side. Mix the cornflour into remaining fat in pan until smooth. Stir in tomato paste and chicken stock. Simmer for 5 minutes. Replace steaks, top with pineapple, and heat through, spooning sauce over during cooking.

BURNER 2. Fry the onions gently in the oil until transparent, add courgettes, salt and herbs and pour in the stock. Cover pan with tight-fitting lid and simmer over heat for about 30 minutes. Remove bouquet garni and serve.

Boeuf Stroganoff

serves 4

Sauté Potatoes

serves 4

A luxurious dish, given here in its original form, which differs from many people's conception of it, but is far superior to the distorted versions often served in restaurants in Britain—and remarkably easy to make.

1½ lb best quality frying steak
1 small onion, *sliced*
½ pint cream
3 oz butter
1 tbspn lemon juice
salt and pepper

1 lb small potatoes
1 oz butter
1 tbspn parsley, *chopped*
½ tspn salt

BURNER 1. Melt the butter and fry the onion over a low heat until golden. Remove and discard. Cut the meat into thick strips about 1½in long and put into the pan. Season and brown briskly on all sides. This should use up most of the butter in the pan. Just as the pan is about to run dry, pour in half a cup of water and stir it round to absorb the congealed juices. Lower heat, stir in cream, then lemon juice. Remove from heat. (Ready soured cream could be used in place of the fresh cream and lemon juice, but is not as good, we think.)

BURNER 2. Scrub the potatoes and boil in salted water for 10 minutes. Drain, cool slightly, peel, and cut lengthwise into slices no thicker than ⅛in. Toss in hot butter until lightly browned, season with salt and serve sprinkled with parsley.

Savoury Minced Beef

serves 4

1 lb minced beef
1 small tin tomatoes
½ pint meat stock
½ tspn chili powder
2 onions, *sliced*
1 stick celery, *cubed*
2 oz butter or fat

Potato Croquettes

serves 4

1 lb potatoes
2 tbspns breadcrumbs
2 oz flour
1 egg
2 oz fat
salt and pepper

BURNER 1. Fry onions over low heat until golden. Add meat, browning quickly. Add remainder of ingredients and simmer for 25 to 30 minutes. Thicken if required.
BURNER 2. Peel, slice, and wash potatoes, and cook in boiling salted water for 15 minutes. Drain, cover pan, and return to low heat to dry them out. Mash, season well, and shape into flat cakes. Pass through flour, beaten egg, and breadcrumbs, and fry in hot fat until golden. Drain well and serve.

Rabbit, Spanish Style

serves 4

1 lb rabbit, *jointed*
4 oz mushrooms, *sliced*
2 Spanish onions, *sliced*
½ lb small ripe tomatoes
2 sticks celery, *sliced*
¾ pint chicken stock
2 oz flour
2 oz fat
2 tbspns vinegar

Macaroni with Cheese

serves 4

6 oz macaroni
1 oz grated cheese
1 oz butter

Dip rabbit joints in vinegar, drain and dust with flour.
BURNER 1. Fry onions and rabbit until golden. Drain off excess fat, add stock, mushrooms and celery. Simmer for at least an hour. Thicken stock with a little flour and then drop in the whole tomatoes and simmer until they are tender but still whole.
BURNER 2. Boil macaroni in salted water until just tender, drain, dot with butter, and serve topped with grated cheese.

Pork Schnitzel

serves 4

4 lean pork chops
1 egg, *beaten*
2 oz breadcrumbs
2 oz flour
4 green olives, *stoned*
8 anchovy fillets
½ lemon, *sliced*
salt and pepper

Sweet and Sour Beetroot

serves 4

2 cooked beetroots, *medium size*
2 tbspns vinegar
2 oz brown sugar
1 oz butter
salt and pepper

Trim meat off bone carefully and cut away excess fat, if any. Place between greaseproof paper and beat flat with anything heavy to hand.
BURNER 1. Flour, egg, and breadcrumb chops and fry both sides until brown. Serve topped with anchovy fillets, slice of lemon and olives.
BURNER 2. Dice beetroots and place in pan over moderate heat with remaining ingredients. Stir until heated through, season well, and serve hot.

Veal Escalopes

serves 4

4 fillets of veal
1 egg, *beaten*
2 oz butter or fat
3 tbspns breadcrumbs
1 tbspn capers
8 anchovy fillets

Savoury Cabbage

serves 4

1 small Savoy cabbage, *shredded*
1 onion, *chopped*
1 cooking apple, *peeled and sliced*
½ pint stock
salt and pepper

Beat the veal out thinly between sheets of greaseproof paper, dip in egg and breadcrumbs.
BURNER 1. Melt the fat and fry the veal for 5 minutes on each side. Garnish with capers and anchovies.
BURNER 2. Place cabbage, onion, and apple in pan, season well, pour in the stock, cover, and cook for 20 minutes.

Lamb Chops with Lemon Sauce

serves 4

4 good size lamb chops
2 oz butter
1 oz flour
½ pint stock
1 tbspn lemon juice
salt and pepper

Peas, Breton Style

serves 4

1½ lb fresh peas
1 onion, *chopped*
½ pint chicken stock
1 tspn sugar
1 oz butter

BURNER 1. Season chops and fry in hot fat until browned on both sides. Put to one side. Stir in flour until smooth. Gradually add stock and lemon juice. Season. Return chops to pan and warm through.
BURNER 2. Place peas and onions in pan, pour on the stock, add the sugar and seasoning, and cook covered for 25 minutes. Remove from heat, drain, add the butter, and shake well.

Grilling on a barbecue

What makes a barbecue exciting to use is probably its antique associations, for next to the open fire this is cooking at its most ancient. The word comes from the French *barbe à queue,* a term that refers to animals roasted whole on a spit, in other words, from head to tail.

A barbecue encourages you to be adventurous since it opens up fascinating new ways of cooking. Meat grilled over charcoal has a unique flavour, of course, but there are many other things you can cook—with the right equipment, you can even bake a cake! And meat that is grilled is the healthiest kind to eat, too.

Portable barbecues on the market, many of them complete with a spit, fold away into a small space. And charcoal in natural or briquette form can be bought almost anywhere. On a grill 12 to 14in across you can cook enough food for four hungry people, more if they are willing to eat in relays. And you can cook several items at once, particularly if you use foil, or keep one dish hot while you get on with another.

Where an open fire would be banned, as on organised camping sites, a barbecue is often allowed. When camping, we use the circular Lucifer, which has a 13in diameter grill, a windshield, a spit for roasting the largest birds, and a cover for smoking fish or for baking. It stays hot for an hour or more on one filling of charcoal. But at home we prefer to build our own barbecue with bricks, wire mesh and an oven rack. We make parallel walls with four bricks each side, lay the mesh over them, then place another row of bricks on top. The oven rack rests on the topmost bricks to serve as a grill, the charcoal on the wire mesh beneath.

Another way is to line flower pots to the brim with foil, half fill them with sand or dry earth and lay the charcoal on this, covering the top with wire mesh on which you grill the food. The Lucifer takes about 2 lb of charcoal at one burning, our home-made barbecue half that—which is just as well, for charcoal is a costly fuel. But in any case, a barbecue is extravagant, for only with top quality meat and other ingredients is it possible to get the best results.

Choose the site for your barbecue carefully, sheltered from the wind and, if you are cooking by day, in the shade. In bright sun it is almost impossible to tell when the fire is ready for cooking. But remember that charcoal fumes are highly dangerous: in an enclosed space they can be fatal.

Pile up the charcoal in the centre of the hearth and light it with paper and wood, or solid fuel Meta tablets. (Better not leave these lying about, by the way, for they are poisonous to humans and pets alike). Never use petrol or any other inflammable liquid to get the fire going. Not only is it a fire risk but it will taint the food, too.

Fan the coals with a piece of stiff card until they begin to glow, then spread them out and cover with more charcoal. You need heat, not flames, for cooking. The fire is ready for grilling (about an hour after being lit) when it is ash grey by day, dull red by night. Either way, it is deceptively hot, so guard against burning your fingers by using tongs for moving the coals and oven mitts or thick gloves for handling the food. Wipe and lightly oil the grill before positioning it over the fire.

Cut the meat into serving size portions, preferably on a nearby table with a heatproof top. Lean tender meat is best for grilling: if you suspect the meat is tough, marinate it overnight first. Steak for the barbecue should be at least 1in thick. Trim off any fat and lightly score the edges with a knife to prevent it curling up during cooking. Steaks large enough for two or three people cook better on the grill than individual ones.

We like our grilled steak crisp on the outside and pink and juicy within. To achieve this, it needs to be about $1\frac{1}{2}$in thick, grilled over a high heat for about 10 minutes, and turned several times during cooking. When you expose meat to high temperatures the liquid on the surface coagulates to form a hermetic seal to prevent any further loss of juice. So we make a point of not oiling or seasoning our meat before grilling it. That way, we retain its juices and avoid the smoke and smell that comes from drops of basting fat falling on the coals. When the top surface starts to bubble turn the meat with a spatula or tongs—never pierce it with a fork or skewer. Then salt and pepper the cooked side.

When preparing kebabs we flavour them with herbs tucked between the pieces of meat. If the herbs are exposed to direct heat their ashes give a bitter taste to the meat. You can perfume the meat almost as well by throwing herbs on the fire a few minutes before taking it off the grill.

Grilling is an excellent way to cook freshwater fish, especially when you stuff them with herbs to bring out the flavour. But score them along the sides first. The skin puts up a barrier to the heat and slows up cooking time. Scoring also allows unwanted fats beneath the skin to escape and stops the fish curling up as the skin shrinks.

Many permutations of kebabs are possible but wise cooks put on the same skewer only items that need the same cooking time. Over a hot fire the outside of an onion, for example, becomes burnt before the inside is cooked. By blanching the vegetables first they can be finished off on the barbecue with meat placed on the same skewer. Or you can cook them on one set of skewers, and the meats on another. We use flat-bladed skewers of stainless steel. Round ones are useless and any other metal is likely to taint the meat. Easiest to use are skewers long enough for their handles to rest outside the fire.

A problem when grilling fat meat, poultry, or fish is how to prevent drops of fat falling on the coals and flaring up to singe the food. The answer is to make a shallow 'pan' from foil, puncture the base at 3in intervals with the tip of a skewer, and lay it on the grill. The holes allow the fat to drain while the meat is grilling.

Use foil in other ways, too. Cook small steaks in it to retain their juices, fry sausages, or grill trout. An ideal way to foil-cook trout is to clean them, remove the heads, stuff with a mixture of butter and herbs, and season the outside. Wrap in foil but leave one end open. Just before placing the foil envelope on the grill pour in half a glass of dry white wine, then seal it up. Cook for 8 minutes on each side.

If the grill of your barbecue is not adjustable, raise heat initially by piling up the coals beneath it, then lower it by spreading them out. On a circular fire the centre is usually the coolest area. To increase the heat temporarily, tap the ash off the coals with your tongs; to reduce it, sprinkle salt or water over the coals.

Meat for grilling should be seasoned after it is cooked, not before. An exception to this rule is chicken grilled on a spit, which needs to be lightly salted before being placed over the fire. (The skin protects the meat from taking up off-flavours and also retains its juices). Salt the inside of the bird, too. Pass the spit through the vent and the neck and truss it tightly, keeping the skin intact. Chicken takes from 40 to 60 minutes to grill, depending on size.

Sole with tarragon

serves 4

4 medium size sole fillets
4 oz butter
2 tbspns olive oil
1 tspn tarragon
juice of 1 lemon
salt and pepper

Wash and dry the fish, then brush lightly with oil and dust on both sides with salt, pepper, and tarragon. Place on hot grill and cook for 4 minutes, turning once. While the fish are cooking, melt butter over the grill and mix it with the lemon juice. Pour over the fish just before serving.

Fish kebabs

serves 4

1½ lb cod fillet
6 oz button mushrooms
1 red pepper, *seeded and halved*
2 rashers back bacon
8 bay leaves
5 fl oz natural yoghourt
1 tspn chili seasoning
½ tspn ground ginger

Cut each rasher into 4 pieces after removing the rind. Skin the fish and cut into cubes. Trim, wash, and dry the mushrooms. Blanch the pepper in boiling water for 3 minutes, drain, and cut into 12 pieces. Blend yoghourt and seasonings. Thread fish, bay leaves, mushrooms, pepper, and bacon onto 8 skewers, brush with the marinade, and place on grill over moderate heat. Cook for about 10 minutes, turning and basting with the marinade several times. Serve with rice or salad. (Apart from thc flavour it imparts, the advantage of using yoghourt for the marinade is that it contains no fat to flare up on the coals).

Grilled trout with almonds

serves 4

4 medium size trout
4 tbspns flour
2 oz butter
2 tbspns flaked almonds
4 tbspns lemon juice
2 tbspns parsley, *chopped*
salt and pepper

Clean and wash the fish and pat dry. Coat them in mixture of flour and seasoning, place on grill, and cook for 15 minutes, turning once. Baste with half the butter. Melt remainder in pan and brown the almonds, stir in lemon juice and parsley and pour over the fish.

Trout with herbs

serves 4

4 medium size trout
4 cloves garlic, *crushed*
2 tbspns olive oil
1 tspn dried mint
½ tspn tarragon
salt and pepper

Clean, wash, and dry the fish, then stuff with the mixture of garlic, herbs, and seasoning. Grill for 15 minutes, turning twice.

Grilled haddock

serves 2

4 small haddock fillets
1 oz butter
1 lemon, *sliced*
salt and pepper

Wipe the fish and place on grill. Melt the butter and have handy near the barbecue. Cook for 2 minutes then turn the fillets and put a teaspoonful of butter on each. Allow the underside to cook for 2 minutes, then turn the fish again, adding butter to the second side. Turn the fish once more. Season and serve with melted butter and slices of lemon. (Basting the fish in this way ensures that the butter will be absorbed and not flare up on the coals).

Chicken supreme

serves 2

2 portions chicken breast
3 tbspns melted butter
1 oz flour
3 tbspns breadcrumbs
1 egg, *beaten*
salt and pepper

Lightly flour the chicken, then drop in beaten egg combined with 1 tablespoon of water. Dust in breadcrumbs, pressing the chicken down with the flat of your hand to ensure that the crumbs adhere. Leave for 1 hour to give time for the egg to set. Dip the supremes in melted butter, drain, and grill for about 8 minutes each side, seasoning the first side only after turning.

Stuffed Steak

serves 2

1 lb fillet steak *1½in thick*
1 shallot, *chopped*
2 cloves garlic, *crushed*
1 tbspn parsley, *chopped*
¼ tspn marjoram
¼ tspn thyme
¼ tspn tarragon
1 oz butter

Cut the steak like a sandwich almost to the opposite edge. Cook the shallot in butter until golden, add the garlic and herbs and mix well over heat. Spread the mixture inside the steak. Handle steak carefully while grilling.

Lamb Kebabs

serves 2

1 lb lamb from top of leg, *cubed*
8 tomatoes
4 medium size onions, *halved*
8 button mushrooms
2 cloves garlic
2 tbspns olive oil
8 bay leaves

Marinate the lamb overnight (see page 59), and blanch the onions in boiling water for 5 minutes. Thread the cubed meat on skewers, concealing half a bay leaf between each cube. On separate skewers thread tomato, onion and mushroom, brush with oil and leave to drain. Grill the meat for 10 minutes. turning frequently. After 5 minutes, place vegetables on grill and cook, turning occasionally until the meat is ready. This is probably the most delicious way to cook lamb.

Hamburgers

serves 4

1 lb minced pork
1 egg, *beaten*
1 small onion, *chopped*
1 tbspn flour
1 tbspn parsley, *chopped*
salt and pepper

Using a fork, mix meat, onion, salt, and pepper in bowl. Drop in the egg and mix again. Pat mixture into equal size cakes ½in thick. Flour lightly. Fry in greased foil over hot coals for 6 minutes, turn and cook for a further 4 minutes.

Foil-baked apples

serves 4

4 large cooking apples
1 oz butter
pinch cinnamon
2 oz apricot jam
2 oz sugar
4 oz cream
yolk of 1 egg

Core but do not peel the apples, score all round their centres with a sharp knife and smear with butter. Mix together in a bowl the sugar, cream, egg yolk, jam and cinnamon. Enclose the apples loosely in aluminium foil, fill the centres with the mixture and close the foil loosely at the top. Place on the grill and cook for 20 minutes.

Saving time with a pressure cooker

As magical as Aladdin's lamp, the pressure cooker has the disadvantage that once you have begun to cook something it is impractical to disturb the process. Timings can be critical too. Yet for the outdoor cook this is a small price to pay for what it makes possible. It cuts cooking time from hours to minutes, produces a full scale meal on only one burner, thereby saving fuel, preserves the vitamin content, flavour, and colour of the food and minimises washing up. It will make the toughest meat unrecognisably tender, can double as an ordinary saucepan, and even be used for deep frying.

We have always found the Prestige 'Skyline' cooker ideal for camping. It is safe (the handgrips make it very easy both to lift or to pack). Accessories include a trivet and a set of separators for cooking different types of food. Cooking time, not quantity of food, determines how much liquid you need, so we always pour this in first to make sure we don't forget it. The liquid must be of the kind that gives off steam: water, milk, or stock—never fat alone, which does not. Unless otherwise instructed for a particular recipe, never use less than ½ pint for the first quarter of an hour and a ¼ pint for each quarter of an hour thereafter. Never fill the cooker more than two-thirds full with solid food, or half full for anything that may rise when coming to the boil. Follow this rule and use a timer so that you know exactly when the cooking time is up, and nothing should go wrong. Each time you cook, check that the control valve is unblocked. Dry the cooker before putting it away and store unsealed to prevent it becoming musty.

Oxtail Stew or Oxtail Soup stew serves 4 soup serves 2-3

Oxtail alone will not provide very substantial portions of meat, but when combined with steak produces a satisfying meat dish as well as delightful gravy.

1 lb oxtail, *cut in pieces*
1 lb stewing steak, *trimmed and cubed (omit for soup)*
3 large onions, *sliced*
1 lb carrots, *sliced*
1 pint rich brown stock
herbs, bayleaf
2 oz beef dripping
1 tbspn tomato paste
½ tbspn lemon juice
1 tbspn flour for thickening
1 tbspn red currant jelly
glass red wine *(optional)*
salt and pepper

Fry onions in hot fat in open cooker. Lift out. Put in well-seasoned meat and brown rapidly all over. Strain off surplus fat, add hot stock, onions, carrots, herbs, bayleaf, tomato paste and lemon juice. Season again and pressure cook for 45 minutes. Leave overnight. Skim off fat. Reheat by bringing to pressure only, cool at air temperature, remove meat and vegetables and keep hot. Add blended flour (wine and jelly) to remaining stock and boil for a few minutes. This dish should be cooked the day before to allow the fat to be skimmed off when cold.

Lamb or Beef Stew

serves 4

$1\frac{1}{2}$ lb lamb, (shoulder or breast) *cubed*
or
$1\frac{1}{4}$ lb stewing steak, *cubed*
1 lb carrots, *sliced*
1 lb onions, *sliced*
$\frac{1}{2}$ pint beef stock
small tin tomatoes
3 large potatoes, *peeled and quartered*
2 oz fat
1 tbspn flour
salt and pepper

Fry onions in melted fat in open cooker, strain off surplus. Add stock and all other ingredients, bring to pressure, and cook for 25 minutes. Reduce pressure with cold water, add flour to thicken, check seasoning, and boil for three minutes in open pan.

Liver and Onions

serves 4

$\frac{3}{4}$ lb liver, *cut in $\frac{1}{2}$in strips*
3 rashers streaky bacon, *diced*
3 onions, *finely sliced*
1 lb small potatoes, *cleaned*
1 small cabbage, *shredded*
$\frac{1}{4}$ pint water or stock
1 tbspn parsley, *chopped*
1 oz fat
1 tbspn flour
salt and pepper

Fry bacon and onions in melted fat in open cooker. Remove and strain off surplus fat. Roll the liver in flour and place the stock, onions, bacon, and seasoning in the base of the cooker and top with the liver. Put in trivet and separators containing the vegetables. Pressure cook for 4 minutes. Reduce pressure with cold water. Serve liver and vegetables and thicken gravy in open cooker by boiling quickly.

Braised Chicken

serves 4

1 chicken (2 to $2\frac{1}{2}$ lb)
4 oz mushrooms, *sliced*
1 small tin tomatoes
2 sticks celery, *chopped*
2 oz cooking fat
$\frac{1}{2}$ pint chicken stock
1 onion stuck with a clove
1 bouquet garni
1 tbspn seasoned flour for thickening

Brown chicken in melted fat in open cooker. Remove chicken and brown vegetables. Place chicken on trivet, add stock and remaining ingredients. Pressure cook for 25 minutes (depending on size of chicken). Reduce pressure at appropriate time if adding rice, potatoes, or other extra vegetables. Serve. Thicken half a cup or so of the remaining stock with the flour and boil in open pan if gravy is required.

Jam Roly Poly

serves 4

6 oz flour
3 oz shredded suet
3 oz jam
pinch salt

Make crust by sieving flour and salt, stirring in suet and adding sufficient water to make an elastic dough. Roll into an oblong, making sure that the width is less than the diameter of the cooker. Spread jam along the centre, wet edges with cold water and roll up lengthwise. Wrap in a cloth lined with greaseproof paper, tie ends securely and drop into $1\frac{1}{2}$ pints of boiling water (adding a little lemon juice to prevent the cooker becoming discoloured). Steam gently for 10 minutes and then cook at pressure for 20 minutes. Reduce at air temperature.

Stewed Dried Fruit

Very easily prepared by using a pressure cooker. Soak, covered in boiling water, for ten minutes before cooking, then add sugar to taste and make up soaking liquid to the amounts given below. Cook for the times specified:

Apple rings	6 minutes	1 pint per lb of fruit
Apricots	3 minutes	$\frac{3}{4}$ pint per lb of fruit
Pears, prunes	10 minutes	1 pint per lb of fruit

ROUGH GUIDE TO COOKING TIMES

Meat	*Time at Pressure*	*Amount of Water*
Boiling:	20-25 minutes for all sizes up to 2 lb in weight (12 minutes per lb)	Ideally just to cover without more than half-filling the pan
Braising:	10-12 minutes per lb	Less than half-covered
Chops and Liver:	7-8 minutes in total	$\frac{1}{2}$ pint
Ham:	12 minutes per lb	$\frac{1}{2}$ pint for 3 lb or less $\frac{1}{4}$ pint for every additional lb
Pot Roasting:	12-15 minutes per lb	$\frac{3}{4}$ pint for joints up to $2\frac{1}{2}$ lb. First brown joint and then cook on trivet
Fish		
Plaice Fillets:	3 minutes on greased trivet	$\frac{1}{2}$ pint (including the 'safety' margin)
Haddock, Cod, Turbot, Halibut:	4 minutes on greased trivet	$\frac{1}{2}$ pint

Fresh Vegetables

	Time at Pressure	*Amount of Water*
Average:	4 minutes	$\frac{1}{2}$ pint (including the 'safety' margin)

Dried Vegetables

Before cooking pour over boiling water and soak for an hour, covered.

Haricot Beans	20 minutes	Make up soaking liquid to 2 pints per lb
Butter Beans	30 minutes	Make up soaking liquid to 2 pints per lb
Lentils	15 minutes	Make up soaking liquid to 2 pints per lb
Split Peas	15 minutes	Make up soaking liquid to 2 pints per lb

Cooking in an oven

An oven has a definite place in cooking in the open air. Outdoor cooks installed in well equipped caravans or boats may have an oven almost as big as the one they use at home.

Many car-borne campers, too, clearly think it worthwhile to include a portable oven in their kitchen equipment. And some adventure campers operating from a fixed base are still attracted to the idea of leaving their evening meal to cook by itself in an old-fashioned haybox before they set off for the day.

A haybox is one in which insulating material, such as dry grass, is packed tightly beneath, around and on top of a cooking pot brought to the boil before being placed in position. If the insulation is adequate, the temperature of the liquid falls only gradually over a long period—during which time the food immersed in it goes on cooking.

Where it would not be practical to carry a box as bulky as this, it is sometimes possible to dig a square hole or build a box shape from stones to serve the same purpose. Or you can buy modern versions of the ancient haybox, too. Nearly as bulky, and not particularly lightweight, they can be used almost anywhere. But no matter how it is made, a haybox does impose a diet of casseroled food not to everyone's taste.

A portable oven will cook much more than that, though it has its drawbacks too. The Kubex we use when camping, made of galvanised steel, functions over most sources of heat to provide a welcome alternative to steamed, boiled or fried food. It does not, however, have the range of a conventional oven, since much of the heat generated at the base escapes through the uninsulated top and sides. But it will bake a satisfactory cake, some breads, and numerous main dishes and desserts—and it folds away into a space no bigger than 12in by 12in by 3in.

The only way you can safely heat a portable oven by gas, however, is on a two-burner hotplate. Even so, it is none too stable and needs to be handled carefully—preferably with thick gloves, if you are to avoid burning your fingers.

We have never tried, but no doubt it is possible to roast a joint of beef in a portable oven. For most of us, though, it would take too long, as would the gentle casseroling of cheaper kinds of meat. In our experience, cooking in an oven of this kind is best confined to smaller cuts or to composite dishes that incorporate meat, recipes for which we give elsewhere.

Name almost any kind of fish, however, and it can be cooked in the oven, in an open dish or enclosed in foil. A whole fish weighing 2 to 3 pounds needs 40 minutes or so in the oven, but smaller pieces would take little more than half that, depending on their thickness.

If you use an oven, get the most out of the fuel it takes to heat it, by cooking as many different dishes as possible in one operation—such as bread or cakes on one shelf, a main dish on another, and a dessert on a third.

Bobotee

serves 4

A South African dish with an unusual flavour, it originated in the kitchens of some of the earliest Dutch settlers.

¾ lb lean pork, *minced*
3 eggs
1½ slices stale bread
⅓ pint milk
1 tbspn butter
1½ tspns curry powder
1 tbspn lemon juice
1 tspn salt
1 clove garlic, *chopped*
¼ tspn pepper
2 tspns granulated sugar
1 onion, *diced*

Fry the onion and garlic in the butter until soft but not browned. Crumble the bread into a mixing bowl and stir in the pork, lemon juice, curry powder, salt, pepper, sugar, 1 whole egg, and all but 3 tablespoons of the milk. Add the onion and garlic and mix thoroughly. Turn the mixture into a greased casserole and bake in a moderate oven for 25 minutes. Lightly beat the remaining two eggs with the remainder of the milk and a pinch of salt. Spoon off any excess fat from the top of the meat, pour in the egg mixture, and bake for another 20 minutes.

Salmon Casserole

serves 4

13 oz tin salmon
3 thick slices bread
1 small onion, *diced*
2 eggs, *beaten*
½ pint tomato juice
3 oz breadcrumbs
3 oz butter
1 tbspn flour
½ tspn salt
¼ tspn mustard
¼ tspn pepper

Bone the salmon and remove the skin, and crumble the bread after discarding the crusts. Melt the butter over a low heat and stir in the flour and tomato juice to form a smooth paste. Allow to cool, then stir in the beaten eggs. Add the fish, crumbled bread, lemon juice, onion, and seasoning and mix thoroughly. Grease a baking dish, sprinkle the breadcrumbs thickly over sides and base, spoon in the mixture, and bake in a moderate oven for 35 minutes or until it is firm and the top has browned.

Savoury Pie

serves 4

12 oz steak, *minced*
½ lb tomatoes, *sliced*
1 oz fat
5 potatoes, *thinly sliced*
3 onions, *sliced*
salt and pepper

Place alternate layers of onion, tomato, and potato in a greased pie dish, season well and cover with the meat. Bake for 45 minutes in a moderately hot oven.

Hungarian Goulash

serves 4

1 lb stewing steak, *cubed*
2 onions, *chopped*
1 small tin tomatoes
1 tspn paprika
¾ pint beef stock
1 oz flour
1 oz fat
1 green pepper, *chopped*
salt and pepper

A dish for the haybox which calls for a heavy cooking pot with a tight fitting lid. Roll meat in seasoned flour, heat the fat and cook onions and pepper together for a few minutes. Add the meat and fry until browned. Stir in tomatoes, a tablespoon of flour, the paprika, and the stock. Cover and bring to the boil, stirring occasionally. Place the pot in the haybox for about $\frac{1}{4}$ hour, take out (cover the box) and bring to a fast boil again. Return it to the box and pack insulating material tightly all round. The stew will be ready to eat any time from 6 to 8 hours after being placed in the box. Serve with boiled potatoes, plain rice or noodles.

Pork Chops, Flemish Style

serves 4

4 pork chops
$\frac{3}{4}$ lb eating apples
1 oz fat
salt and pepper

Season chops and fry in hot fat until brown on both sides. Place apples in an earthenware dish, lay the chops on top, sprinkle with a little fat, and cook in oven for 25 to 35 minutes.

Chicken Casserole

serves 4 to 5

1 $2\frac{1}{2}$ lb chicken
$\frac{1}{2}$ pint chicken stock
1 onion, *sliced*
1 carrot, *sliced*
1 stick celery, *sliced*
1 oz butter
1 bouquet garni
salt and pepper

Put vegetables in bottom of casserole. Season chicken and place on top. Spread butter over chicken. Cover and cook in fairly hot oven for $\frac{3}{4}$-1 hour, until chicken is tender. Take out. Skim off fat, add stock, and heat up, thickening if necessary. Strain liquid over the chicken and serve.

Loin Chop Toad-in-the-Hole

serves 4

4 pork loin chops
1 oz dripping
$\frac{1}{4}$ pint milk and water mixed
4 oz plain flour
1 small egg
$\frac{1}{4}$ tspn salt

Make the batter and allow to stand for at least half an hour if possible. Put chops in roasting dish with dripping and put in oven for 5 minutes to seal. Pour batter over and cook for 35 minutes. In place of the chops use 1 lb sausages, in which case heat fat, pour in batter and then pop in sausages. Bake for 35-40 minutes.

Ten Minute Pie

serves 3 to 4

4 oz ham or bacon, *diced*
2 tomatoes, *skinned and sliced*
3 slices bread
salt and pepper
4 eggs, *separated*
1 oz cheese, *grated*
1 oz butter

Cut the bread into triangles after removing the crusts and place in a greased baking dish. Sprinkle ham or bacon over them and cover with tomatoes dotted with butter. Beat egg yolks and cheese together and season well. Whip egg whites until stiff, fold into yolk and cheese mixture, and pour over the tomatoes. Bake in moderate oven until the eggs are set (about 10 minutes).

Oatmeal biscuits

makes 15

3 oz oatmeal
7 oz flour
3 oz caster sugar
1 egg
¼ tspn baking powder
3 oz butter
1 cup water

Mix dry ingredients, melt butter and stir in. Beat egg with tablespoon of cold water and add to mixture. Mix well and turn onto floured board. Roll out thinly and cut into rounds. Place on greased baking sheet or foil and bake in hot oven for 20 minutes.

Cornish pasties

makes 4

8 oz frozen short pastry
4 oz raw potato, *finely diced*
4 oz beef or lamb
yolk of 1 egg
1 onion, *chopped*
salt and pepper

Cut the meat up small. Roll out the pastry and cut into four rounds of equal size. Mix meat, onion, and potato together, moisten with a little stock or water and season well. Place a quarter of the mixture in the centre of each round, fold the pastry over, and seal the edges firmly. Brush the pasties with beaten egg yolk (or milk) and cook in moderate oven for 1 hour.

Oven-baked Pizza

serves 2

6 oz flour
2 tspns baking powder
1 small tin Italian tomatoes
4 tbspns Cheddar cheese, *grated*
2 tbspns olive oil
½ cup water
4 anchovy fillets
½ tspn oregano or basil
salt and pepper

Heat the oven and grease a baking sheet with half the oil. Put the flour on a board, make a well in the centre, add the baking powder and ½ teaspoon of salt and mix with water to make a stiff dough. Knead lightly then roll out to a ¼ in-thick round. Place on baking tray. Spread the tomatoes over the dough, season with salt and pepper, decorate with anchovies and cover with the cheese. Sprinkle oregano or basil on top and pour on the remainder of the oil. Bake in moderate oven for 15 to 20 minutes. (If you prefer, use frozen shortcrust pastry for the base if available).

Cheesecake

8 oz frozen short pastry
2 oz caster sugar
juice and rind of 1 lemon
8 oz cream cheese (or curd)
2 eggs, *separated*
2 oz sultanas

Separate the egg yolks and put the whites to one side. Grate the lemon rind and squeeze the juice. Line a flan case with the rolled out pastry. Beat together the cheese, egg yolks, sugar and juice and rind of the lemon, then stir in the sultanas. Whisk egg whites until stiff and fold in. Pour the mixture into the pastry case and bake for 30 minutes or until the filling is firm.

Easy Quiche

8 oz frozen short pastry
2 oz butter
2 onions, *finely sliced*
$\frac{1}{3}$ pint milk
8 oz curd cheese
2 eggs
2 rashers bacon, *diced*
2 tbspns Cheddar cheese, *grated*

Line an 8in flan case with the rolled out pastry. Fry onions and bacon in butter until the onions are transparent. Beat curd cheese. milk, and eggs together, mix in grated cheese, bacon, and onion and pour into pastry case. Bake in moderate oven for 25 minutes. The quiche is cooked if you push the point of a knife into the filling and it comes out clean.

Mock Cheese Soufflé

This dish needs to be made up well in advance since the ingredients must be soaked for at least 5 hours. It is satisfactory and reliable substitute for a genuine soufflé.

6 slices stale bread
6 slices of cheese
1 pint milk
2 oz butter
salt and pepper

Remove crusts from bread, and butter the slices on one side. Lay two slices, buttered side down, in greased baking tin or oven proof dish. Cover bread with two slices of cheese, add two more slices of bread, buttered side down, next a layer of cheese and then a final layer of of bread and cheese. Pour in enough milk to cover. Leave to stand for 5 to 6 hours, then spoon out any excess milk, season well and bake in moderate oven for 45 minutes. When cooked, the mixture will have puffed up and the top become a glossy brown.

Banana Pudding

serves 4

3 bananas, *sliced*
1 oz custard powder
grated rind of 1 lemon
4 slices stale bread
$1\frac{1}{4}$ pints milk
1 oz sugar

Boil the milk, break bread into small pieces, and pour $\frac{1}{2}$ pint milk over. Add lemon rind and leave to stand until the bread is soft. Make the custard, using $\frac{3}{4}$ pint of milk, sugar and custard powder. Beat the bread mixture well, then stir in the custard. Butter a pie dish, put in the bananas and then the custard mixture. Bake until the top has browned (about 20 minutes). Sprinkle with sugar and serve.

Vanilla Soufflé Omelette

serves 4

3 eggs, *separated*
$1\frac{1}{2}$ oz sugar
1 tbspn caster sugar
$\frac{1}{4}$ tspn salt
3 drops vanilla essence

Separate the eggs. Butter an oven dish and sprinkle with caster sugar. Beat egg yolks with the sugar and vanilla until fluffy, whisk salt and egg whites until stiff, and fold in. Pour into dish and bake in moderate oven for 15 to 20 minutes.

Apples and Raisins

serves 4

4 large cooking apples
1 cup raisins
1 glass white wine
1 oz butter
1 oz sugar

Soak raisins in hot water for 1 hour. Core apples but do not peel. Fill centre of each apple with raisins sprinkled with sugar and topped by knob of butter. Place apples in ovenproof dish, pour in the wine and cook in moderate oven for 20 to 25 minutes.

Sauces and dressings

Sauces add splendour to cooking by providing contrasts of taste and texture that enhance great dishes and transform humble ones. Serve them with the appropriate sauce and even left-overs can be appetizing —and since sauces can be made quickly with the minimum of equipment, they are perfectly practicable for cooks operating out of doors.

Where possible, every sauce should contain elements of the dish with which you intend to serve it; the stock from boiled or poached fish, the congealed juices from fried or grilled meat. If what you cook, however, produces little or no natural stock, you can use yeast extract or meat cubes for meat sauces, anchovy essence for fish sauces, or chicken stock cubes for poultry (which go well with pork, too). These may not always fill the bill, however, in which case you can make an appropriate sauce of your own, using Bechamel as a foundation. This is the grandmother of all white sauces; simple, with few ingredients.

Bechamel Sauce

2 tbspns butter
½ pint milk
pinch nutmeg
2 tbspns flour
salt and pepper

Warm the milk. Melt the butter and as soon as it begins to foam remove from heat and stir in the flour (preferably sifted first) and then a little of the warmed milk. Return to the heat and gradually add the rest of the milk. Season with salt, pepper and a pinch of nutmeg and simmer for at least 10 minutes to give time for the flour to cook (the reason why some sauces taste floury is because the flour has not been given time to cook). Stir continuously to eliminate any lumps. There's no need to worry, though, since you can always strain it at the end.

Bechamel forms the basis of many other sauces, all easily made. Here are a few of them, suitably adapted.

Sauce Aurore: serve with eggs, shrimps, prawns, and other seafood. To the basic Bechamel add 3 tablespoons of tomato juice, or diluted tomato ketchup (not purée) and a dash of lemon juice. For a richer sauce, add as much cream as you can spare (at least 3 tablespoons), ½ tspn anchovy essence, black pepper, a tablespoon of lemon juice and a dash of cognac.

Sauce Mornay: serve with vegetables. Add to Bechamel 4 tablespoons grated Gruyere or Parmesan cheese, ½ chicken cube melted in 2 tablespoons of cream and seasoned with pepper and nutmeg. Alternatively make a simple sauce by adding grated cheese and ½ teaspoon dry mustard to the Bechamel.

Rapid Mayonnaise (1)

1 egg
1 tspn vinegar
1 tbspn lemon juice
½ pint olive oil
¼ tspn pepper
¼ tspn dry mustard
1 tspn salt

A thinner, less rich mayonnaise than the conventional kind, which most people will prefer.

Put whole egg (yolk and white) into a small deep bowl with the vinegar, mustard, salt and pepper. Beat for 30 seconds. Add the oil—half a teacupfull at a time if you like—beating for 30 seconds after each addition. (The amount of oil depends upon the size of egg used). If the mayonnaise is still not stiff enough for your liking slowly add more oil, a tablespoon at a time. Then add the lemon juice.

Rapid Mayonnaise (2)

yolks of 2 hardboiled eggs
yolk of 1 raw egg
½ tbspn vinegar
½ tspn made mustard
½ pint olive oil
salt and pepper

Add a few drops of vinegar to the hard boiled yolks and mash to as smooth a paste as time or energy permits. Stir in the raw egg yolk and the rest of the seasoning, then add the oil. We add it in two stages and stir vigorously for a few seconds in between. By adding a tablespoon of tomato juice or diluted ketchup, a dash of lemon juice and a pinch of paprika the mayonnaise becomes a magnificent dressing for a shrimp, lobster or crab cocktail.

For Sauce Verte (Green Sauce), strain spinach into the mayonnaise, add a tablespoon of lemon juice and more pepper. Magnificent with salmon.

For Tartare Sauce, add finely chopped capers, gherkins and a teaspoon of mixed parsley, tarragon, and chervil.

French Dressing (Vinaigrette)

A perfect dressing for salads, whether mixed, green, cooked or fresh.

1 tbspn white or wine vinegar
3 tbspns oil
1 clove garlic, *crushed*
pinch mustard and pepper
¼ tspn salt

Cream the garlic with the salt and mix with the mustard, vinegar, and pepper. Add the oil, stir, and adjust seasoning as necessary. If the dressing has not blended thoroughly, add a little more salt. If it is too sharp, add a little sugar.

Sour Cream Dressing

A useful alternative to French dressing, and one easy to make:

¼ pint sour cream
2 tbspns lemon juice
1 level tbspn sugar
¼ tspn paprika

For a lighter dressing replace the cream with yoghourt.
Mix all the ingredients together and beat until the mixture is reasonably thick and smooth.

Marinades for Grilling

Olive oil and an acid liquid like lemon juice or dry white wine are the basis of most marinades for meat grilled on a barbecue or over an open fire. Make them aromatic by adding either garlic, onion, thyme, sweet marjoram, basil, rosemary, or clove, all of which need to be crushed to render up their perfume. Don't mix too many together, but aim rather for a dominant flavour.

Not only does marinading help to tenderise meat but the oil also impregnates it, so when being grilled marinaded meat does not need to be basted—thereby eliminating the smoke and smell that arises when drops of fat fall on the fire.

Marinade for Lamb

$\frac{1}{4}$ pint olive oil
juice of $\frac{1}{2}$ lemon
$\frac{1}{4}$ pint wine vinegar
$\frac{1}{2}$ tspn rosemary
1 tspn dried oregano
1 tomato, *crushed*
1 onion, *chopped*
1 bayleaf
salt and pepper

Mix in a large bowl, put in lamb, and leave to marinate for 24 hours.

Marinade for Steak

$\frac{1}{2}$ cup olive oil
3 cloves garlic, *crushed*
2 tbspns lemon juice

Mix the ingredients together in a large bowl. Marinate steaks in a cool place for 12 hours, turning several times. Dry the meat with kitchen paper and remove any traces of garlic adhering to it.

Marinade for Fish

$\frac{1}{2}$ cup olive oil
juice of $\frac{1}{2}$ lemon
$\frac{1}{2}$ tspn thyme

Leave the slices of fish in the marinade for one to two hours, turning several times. Wipe the fish dry before grilling.

Simple Barbecue Sauce

1 tin tomatoes
1 tbspn olive oil
1 onion, *chopped*
1 tbspn white wine
1 tbspn vinegar
salt and pepper

Fry the onion in the oil until transparent, mix in remaining ingredients and simmer for 5–10 minutes.

Simple cold desserts

No meal is really complete without a sweet course. That is even more true, perhaps, out of doors than at home. Children especially burn up more energy than usual in the open air and for them the dessert is often the part of the meal they look forward to the most. Fresh fruits are probably the most obvious choice in summer. But why not make them more interesting by combining two or more varieties, or bring out their flavour by dressing them with an appropriate sauce?

Desserts don't have to be complicated, or take a long time to prepare. Some can be ready in minutes, some can be made the day before, and many need no cooking at all.

Chestnut Soufflé

serves 4

1 tin chestnut purée
½ pint double cream

Whip together and serve.

Fresh Fruit Salad

serves 4

1 apple, *chopped*
1 orange, *peeled*
1 pear, *sliced*
4 oz grapes
1 small melon, *peeled and cubed*
3 tbspns red wine
2 oz sugar

This makes a somewhat luxurious salad, though you can vary the ingredients more or less as you like.

Mix fruit together in a bowl. Sprinkle with sugar and pour over wine. Chill if possible before serving.

Apricot Pudding

serves 4

1 large (1 lb 13 oz) tin apricots
1 packet of sponge fingers
1 tbspn lemon juice
½ oz gelatine
2 oz sugar

Line a basin with the sponge fingers, packing them as closely together as possible. Drain apricots, reserve the juice, and fill centre of basin with fruit. Make up juice to one pint, add sugar and lemon juice. Dissolve gelatine in 2 tbspn water and set aside to soak for a few minutes, then stir into the reserved juice. Pour all but a little of the juice over the apricots in the basin, cover the top with more sponge fingers and add remaining juice. Put a weighted plate on top and leave to set, preferably overnight. Serve with fresh cream.

Blackcurrant Jelly

serves 4

1 lb ripe blackcurrants
4 oz caster sugar
1 pint water
2 level tbspns cornflour

Wash currants but do not bother to stalk them as you can sieve them later. Cook with water and sugar until soft. Rub through a sieve together with the liquid. Mix cornflour to a smooth paste with a little water, add to juice and cook for 10 minutes, stirring constantly. Turn into wet mould and leave to set. Serve with milk or cream. Alternative fruits are blackberries, gooseberries, bilberries (add more sugar), damsons (much more sugar).

Coffee Cream

serves 2

½ pint milk
2 eggs, ***beaten***
½ cup strong coffee
few drops vanilla essence
4 oz cream (or small tin evaporated milk)
½ oz gelatine
2 oz sugar

Dissolve the gelatine in half the milk, bring remainder to boil and pour very slowly over beaten egg. Add sugar. Place in double saucepan (or bowl over hot water) and stir until the mixture begins to thicken. Remove from heat and when lukewarm strain in the vanilla and gelatine very gradually, keeping the mixture smooth. Allow to cool. Whip cream (or milk) until stiff, add the coffee and stir gently into the custard. Leave to set.

Greengage Fool

serves 4

1 lb greengages
¼ pint cream
4 oz sugar
2 tbspns water

Stew the greengages over a low heat to a pulp with the sugar and water. Rub through a sieve. When cold, whip cream and mix in.

Summer Pudding

serves 4

½ lb raspberries or blackberries
½ lb gooseberries or blackcurrants
6 oz sugar
4 thick slices of bread
¼ pint water

Remove the crusts from the bread, clean, wash, and stalk the fruit and simmer with water and sugar till soft. Line a basin with the bread, fitting the slices as neatly together as you can and cutting a round to fit the base. Reserve ½ cup of the juice and pour fruit and remainder of juice into basin. Fit slices of bread over top and pour over reserved juice. Place a weighted plate on top and leave overnight to set.

Chocolate Blancmange

serves 4

1 pint milk
1½ oz cornflour
2 oz grated chocolate
1½ oz sugar

Mix the cornflour, chocolate, and sugar to a thin paste with a little of the milk. Boil the remainder and pour slowly over the mixture, stirring all the time. Return to pan and simmer gently for 5 minutes, stirring continuously. Turn into a wet mould to set.

Apple Snow

serves 4

1 lb cooking apples
1 egg white
4 glacé cherries
juice of 1 lemon
1 tbspn caster sugar

Peel, core, and slice the apples. Cook with only a little water until tender. Mash them, add lemon juice, and beat to a thick cream. Add egg white and beat until fluffy. Decorate with a glacé cherry.

Zabaglioni

serves 4

Yolks of 4 eggs
2 oz caster sugar
pinch of salt
2 tbspns Marsala, Brown Sherry, or Madeira

Whisk egg yolks, salt and sugar together and then add the wine. Stand basin over very hot water and whisk until the mixture becomes three times its original bulk. You may like to fold in carefully at the end ¼ pint of lightly whipped cream.

Melon Surprise

serves 4

4 small canteloupe melons
1 lb strawberries
4 oz caster sugar
4 tbspns brandy or liqueur

Wash and quarter the strawberries. Slice off the tops of the melons and put to one side. Leaving the shell intact, cut round the flesh with a grapefruit knife, scoop out and cut into small pieces. Fill the shell with alternate layer of melon, sugar, and strawberries. Pour over the brandy or liqueur and replace the top. Serve chilled if possible.

Strawberry Orange

serves 4 to 6

2 lb strawberries
4 oranges
4 oz caster sugar
juice of ½ lemon

Wash and dry the strawberries, pile them up in the centre of a dish, and pour over the juice of two oranges and half a lemon. Dust with sugar and decorate with slices of orange.

Chocolate Banana Cream

serves 4

4 bananas
8 oz cream
3 oz caster sugar
1 lemon
2 oz plain chocolate

Mash the bananas in a bowl and stir in the sugar and lemon juice. Beat the cream until stiff, add to the banana mixture and pour into individual glasses. Top with grated chocolate.

Fruit Layer Pudding

serves 6

1 melon
3 peaches
2 oranges
3 apples
4 oz caster sugar
1 oz butter

Wash and stone the peaches, halve the melon and remove peel and pips, peel and core the apples and peel the oranges. Cut the fruit up small but keep it separate. Butter a deep bowl and arrange the fruit in layers about 2 inches deep, dusting each layer liberally with sugar before adding the next. Continue until the bowl is full. Cover, put a heavy weight on top, and leave overnight. What fruit you use is unimportant, so long as their flavours contrast with each other.

Index